Caribbean

Ports of Call

Front cover: Pink Sands
Beach, Harbour Island,
Bahamas

Right: cruising the Caribbean

The Cockscomb Basin Wildlife Sanctuary and Jaguar Preserve, Belize You may be lucky enough to spot a jaguar here *(page 53)*

Pirates of the Caribbean •
The Caribbean's seafaring history is revealed at the Pirates of Nassau Museum in the Bahamas *(page 61)*

The Grenadines
Snorkelling and diving here second to none *(page 151)*

Les Chutes du Carbet, Guadeloupe Hike through the forest and see the highest waterfall in the Caribbean *(page 117)*

Chichén Itzá ○ Magical Maya ruins such as the Pyramid of Kukulcán (El Castillo) are the highlight of any visit to the Yucatán, Mexico *(page 47)*

Costa Rica ○ Tropical rainforests, gushing rivers and rare wildlife make this a popular destination *(page 56)*

Surfer's Paradise ○ Atlantic rollers at Bathsheba in Barbados *(page 146)*

The Pitons ○ St Lucia's dramatic landmark peaks dominate the landscape at Soufrière *(page 134)*

River Rafting ○ A great way to travel in Jamaica *(page 81)*

Eagle Beach ○ On the northwest coast of Aruba, this idyllic beach is one of the Caribbean's best *(page 165)*

A PERFECT CRUISE

Day 1 Barbados

Arrive a day before the cruise and explore Barbados. Take a jeep safari round the island, visiting the windswept beaches along the rugged Atlantic coast, or walk around Bridgetown, with its British influence and impressive Parliament building, and the nearby historic Garrison area. Board the ship late afternoon and raise a glass as the Captain sets a course for the Grenadines.

Day 3 St Lucia and Castries

Be on deck early as the ship approaches Soufrière, in the shadow of the dramatic Pitons, a stunning sight in the early morning light. Take a tour of St Lucia's wild side: the world's only drive-in volcano and the Diamond Waterfall, cascading over lush tropical foliage. In the afternoon, check out Castries with its arty vibe – there are some great galleries selling batik, silk screens, sculpture, oils and watercolours, or try the Craft Market for local souvenirs.

Day 4 St-Barths

Step ashore amidst some of the most lavish private yachts to be found in the Caribbean. Stroll around Gustavia, the chic capital, or from the port, walk to pretty Shell Beach which is overlooked by a cool Brazilian bar. On the way back to the dock, have a drink at Le Select, a lively yachtie pub.

Day 2 Mayreau, Grenadines

From the dock at tiny Mayreau, jump on a charter boat to the uninhabited Tobago Cays for some of the best snorkelling in the Caribbean. Exotic coloured fish dart in and out of the coral and the visibility is astonishing.

IN THE CARIBBEAN

Day 6   Virgin Gorda (BVI)

Spend the day splashing around at The Baths, one of the most beautiful beaches in the Caribbean, a jumble of giant boulders scattered on soft, white sand, creating secluded pools and cool caves.

Day 5   St-Martin

Wander around the little town of Marigot, capital of the French side of the island, complete with boulangerie. At lunchtime, take a taxi to Grand Case, a single street along the shore lined with some of the finest restaurants in the Caribbean. Grab a waterside table at L'Escapade, choose your lobster, order a glass of chilled rosé, and don't move until sunset.

Day 9   Miami

If you're on an evening flight back to Europe, disembark from the ship, check in at the airport and then head to South Beach and the city's Art Deco district. A spot of lunch later, followed by a stroll on the beach and shopping, and you'll be in relaxed mood for that flight home.

Day 7–8   All at sea

Two blissful days to bask by the pool with a book, or attend a lecture, try a class or indulge yourself in the on-board spa. Keep an eye out for dolphins and whales racing the ship at sunrise and sunset.

CONTENTS

Introduction 11

Where to Go 21

⚓► *Anchor symbol denotes a port of call*

Sailing out of America 21

*Miami 21, Fort Lauderdale 28, Port Canaveral 31,
Orlando Theme Parks 34, Tampa 34, New Orleans
35, Galveston 36, Houston 37, Key West 37*

Mexico and Central America 41

*Cozumel 42, Cancún 44, Playa del Carmen 44,
Costa Maya 48, Belize 51, Honduras 54, Costa
Rica 56*

The Bahamas 59

*New Providence Island 59, Paradise Island 62,
Grand Bahama 62*

The Western Caribbean 67

*Cuba 67, Grand Cayman 69, Jamaica 73,
Dominican Republic 81, Puerto Rico 83*

The Eastern Caribbean 87

*US Virgin Islands 87, British Virgin Islands 94, Sint
Maarten 97, St-Martin 99, St-Barthélemy 100,
St Kitts 103, Nevis 106, Antigua 107, Guadeloupe
112, Dominica 118, Martinique 124, St Lucia 131,
Barbados 138*

The Southern Caribbean 147

*St Vincent and The Grenadines 148, Grenada 151,
Trinidad and Tobago 158, Aruba and Curaçao 163*

10

166

44

A–Z Travel Tips 170

Choosing a Cruise 171

Theme Cruises 172, Choosing a Cabin 174, Weddings 176

Preparing for the Trip 177

Booking a Cruise 177, Counting the Cost 178, Health 179, When to Go 181

Life on Board 182

Activities and Entertainment 183, Etiquette 184, Food and Drink 184, Ship Facilities 185

Life on Shore.................... 187

Shore Excursions 187

Cruise Line Information 187

Tourist Information 189

Index 190

Features

How to be a Savvy Sailor. 17
USA 22
Hemingway's Home. 38
Mexico. 40
Central America. 52
San Blas Islands 56
The Bahamas. 58
The Western Caribbean 66
The Eastern Caribbean. 88
Best Beaches. 99
Whale Watching in Dominica 122
The Southern Caribbean 154
Carnival in Trinidad. 159
Venezuelan Ports of Call 167
Cruising and the Environment. 169

96

77

67

CRUISING THE CARIBBEAN

Douglas Ward, the world's leading authority on cruise ships, considers why many people choose to cruise the Caribbean

The tropical islands of the Caribbean – the West Indies – arc down from the southern Florida coast to Venezuela like a jewelled necklace, often within sight of one another. Each island has a character, atmosphere and flavour of its own, shaped by its history and its people. Embracing the vast Caribbean basin on its western shores are Mexico and the Central American countries and between them all they offer sandy beaches, turquoise and blue waters, coral reefs, bougainvillea, rainforests, exotic fruits, glowing sunshine, vibrant music, vivid history and friendly, laid-back people. So it's no wonder the countries of the Caribbean are among the most popular holiday destinations.

There was a time when just getting to the region was an adventure; now the adventure can start on a cruise, and travelling on a luxury floating hotel is a wonderful way to experience the atmosphere of the Caribbean, particularly for first-time visitors.

Nowhere in the world is there such a wide collection of exotic islands and countries to which ships, including the largest ones, can travel. With many cruises beginning in Florida, San Juan, Puerto Rico, or in Barbados, much of the region is accessible on rela-

Island hibiscus

tively short trips by sea, and the value for money is unbeatable. Today, cruising is not just for the older, wealthy few – passengers come from all age groups and walks of life, and cruises are designed to suit their different needs. The virtually crime-free environment is particularly attractive to families.

Cruising has come a long way since the 'booze cruises' of the 1930s, designed chiefly to escape Prohibition laws in the United States. The industry launched the revival of fortunes for many Caribbean islands, but World War II intervened and it was only in the 1960s that cruising was reborn, with passengers being flown to embarkation ports, and a working relationship emerging between cruise lines and airlines.

Most ships started in Miami and went no further than the Bahamas, the US Virgin Islands and maybe San Juan, on itineraries that lasted a week – still the favourite duration for most passengers, but the lines soon realised that they needed new ports and new islands to visit.

First, they sent their ships west to Mexico's Yucatán Peninsula, to Cozumel and Playa del Carmen (in reach of the Maya ruins), and then they turned south. But to get down south and see more than just one or two islands would take longer than a week if a ship started in Miami or another Florida port, so the cruise lines started to base ships at islands such as Barbados. One of the bonuses of starting and ending a cruise in a Caribbean port is that a holiday can be extended by staying an extra week on the island.

The worldwide cruise industry has grown enormously since then; the concept hasn't changed much but it has been vastly improved, refined, expanded and packaged. Ten companies operating large ships (loosely defined as ships carrying between 2,500 and 5,400 passengers) dominate the market, but smaller vessels (carrying fewer than 700 passengers) also have a place, able to enter the uncrowded harbours where their larger sisters cannot venture.

INTRODUCTION

The whole of the Caribbean region has had a turbulent and extremely varied history. You will notice on arrival at any island port that there is at least one fortress guarding the harbour mouth, or perched up on a hillside with a panoramic view of the sea.

These scattered vestiges of military power, some ruined and others restored, remind us that the Caribbean has always been fought over. Its landscapes are marked not only by fortifications, but by reminders of battles, uprisings and massacres. The surrounding seas have witnessed countless naval engagements and they conceal a wealth of sunken warships, rusting cannons – and treasure.

Not only did competing European nations go to war over this rich and desirable region, fighting out their quibbles from home on this glorious sea, but pirates preyed on its ports, and African slaves rose up in violent bids for freedom. Only in more recent times have these islands discovered peace.

Early Conquests

The first people to discover the Caribbean were Amerindians who, thousands of years ago, travelled here in dug-out canoes from the Orinoco Basin in Venezuela, peacefully settling the islands. Around AD1000 the Carib Indians paddled up in canoes from the same jungle area of South America and ousted the inhabitants and the region was named after them.

The Carib invasion may have been violent, but it was mild in comparison to the horrors inflicted by the first European invaders. Backed by the Spanish monarchy, Christopher Columbus arrived 500 years later, thinking he had reached the

Maracas beach, Trinidad

Privateers

Notorious pirates such as Henry Morgan and Edward 'Blackbeard' Teach were independent operators, attacking Spanish ships, smuggling and slave-trading, until they were sponsored by European rulers at home, and renamed privateers.

East Indies, and heralded the start of the conquest by Europeans of the West Indies and the New World. He was closely followed by Spanish conquistadors in pursuit of gold. Greed for this precious metal drove the Spanish to colonise the larger islands of Hispaniola, Cuba and Puerto Rico, and they brutally forced the Amerindians to search for it. They in turn succumbed to European diseases or were killed in uprisings. From here, the Spanish went on to Mexico and Central America, where they discovered the treasures of the Maya civilizations. Lacking gold, the smaller Eastern Caribbean islands were not colonised until sugar was introduced.

European Battles

Other European nations watched the expansion of the Spanish Caribbean with keen interest. Protestant England was hostile towards Catholic Spain and Sir Francis Drake attacked and occupied Santo Domingo in Hispaniola, in 1585, destroying the pride of the Spanish Empire. At the same time pirates, such as Henry Morgan and Edward 'Blackbeard' Teach, began to prey on Spanish galleons and ports. In response, the Spanish fortified their towns and protected their fleets with warships.

Gradually, other European nations began to settle in the region. The English claimed St Kitts in 1624 and Barbados in 1627. The French took Martinique and Guadeloupe in 1635 and the Dutch took six Antillean islands between 1630 and 1640.

Throughout the 17th and 18th centuries, the European powers sent their fleets to battle for control of the West Indies and its rich sugar industry. The British took Jamaica from the Spanish in 1655 and did their utmost to weaken the Spaniards' dominance of the larger islands. At the same time, conflicts between the British, French and Dutch reflected wider hostilities in Europe. No sooner were peace treaties signed than a new outbreak of fighting shook the region. Between 1660 and 1814, the island of St Lucia changed hands between the British and French 14 times. During this period, millions of enslaved Africans were brought to the islands to ensure the flow of sugar to Europe was not interrupted.

Sugar and Slavery

The sugar industry reached its zenith in the second half of the 18th century, the age of luxurious 'great houses' and

Workers cutting sugar cane at Montego, 1900

Statue acknowledging the country's past, in Puerto Rico

fantastically rich West Indian planters. Fabulous fortunes were made, both by planters and manufacturers and traders in Europe.

The single event that changed the course of Caribbean history was the slave revolution of 1791–1804, which destroyed the French colony of Saint Domingue and created the independent republic of Haiti. The other Caribbean societies watched with horror as the region's richest colony disintegrated. Another blow to 'King Sugar came with the development of a rival beet sugar industry in Europe. European farmers and manufacturers began to compete with the vested interests of the old 'plantocracy'.

Slavery was eventually abolished during the mid-19th century (it took longest to disappear in the Spanish colonies). Contract labourers arrived from India and other countries to fill the gaps left by the departing slaves. But the industry went through hard times, and gradually the European powers lost interest in their Caribbean possessions.

Roads to Independence

As the 20th century dawned, what most of the Caribbean islands wanted was independence. Haiti proclaimed its independence in 1804, but had been plagued by instability and poverty. The Dominican Republic finally threw out the

Spanish in 1864; Cuba and Puerto Rico followed suit in 1898.

But American influence had taken hold in the larger islands of the Western Caribbean, creating resentment among those who wanted to be free of outside interference. Afraid of communism, the US supported conservatives, including such unsavoury dictators as Rafael Leonidas Trujillo, who ran the Dominican Republic like a family business from 1930 to 1961. Washington's worst fears were realised when another dictator, Fulgencio Batista of Cuba, was ousted in 1959, and replaced by the revolutionary, later Communist, government of Fidel Castro.

Mostly, independence took a more peaceful form. The British colonies were given independence from the 1960s onwards, though some preferred to maintain their links with Europe. In 1946, Martinique and Guadeloupe voted to become *départements* of France, while the Dutch islands formed a federation with the Netherlands.

A few tiny territories, such as Montserrat, the Turks and Caicos and Anguilla, opted to remain British, rather than face the economic uncertainty of independence.

The Caribbean Today

In many respects, the modern Caribbean is something of a success story. With the exception of Cuba, the region mostly enjoys democratic government and a steadily growing standard of living. Barbados, for instance, has some of the best quality-of-life statistics outside Europe and North America. But there are still

Happy Trinidadians

Cruise ships in St-Martin

social and political flashpoints in the region. Cuba's future remains uncertain, and Haiti's deep-seated problems seem no closer to a solution. There is occasional trouble in the tough inner-city ghettos of Kingston, Jamaica, and elections in Trinidad have been tense to say the least.

However, the threats facing the Caribbean today are now more economic than political. As a cluster of small states, the islands are especially vulnerable to developments beyond their control. These range from the hurricanes that regularly ravage communities, to globalisation and the loss of export markets to cheaper producers around the world. But in the true Caribbean spirit, the islanders will not be beaten while the land and sea around them can still provide them with a livelihood in the form of tourism. The importance of this industry cannot be overstated, some 3 million jobs depend on tourism and it is estimated that more than US$40 billion comes into the region through tourist spending.

People who depend on the influx of tourists don't just work in the hotels and retaurants, they include farmers, taxi drivers and artisans.

Caribbean Cruising

The typical attractions of the Caribbean need no introduction and cruise ships offer a particularly inviting way into this rich and varied part of the world. In a week, for instance, it is possible to explore half a dozen entirely different islands, getting a tantalising taste of the Caribbean's diversity. In some cases, a day may be long enough to gain an impression of an island, especially if it's a small one. A brief visit may leave you wanting to see more, 85 percent of cruise passengers come back, and many people return for a longer stay in a place they first visited on a cruise ship.

The beauty of Caribbean cruising is that each day offers an entirely different cultural experience. At first sight, some

How to be a Savvy Sailor

First time cruisers may find it bewildering at the start of a cruise, but those who have been before won't hang around discussing the size of their cabin (they are all small) but will get down to organising their leisure pursuits. Savvy sailors know to arrive at the harbour early and to embark as soon as possible. While others are waiting for their luggage to be taken to the stateroom (it takes hours), well-practised cruisers are moving from deck to deck, swiftly securing the best of everything. First they book any exciting sounding shore excursions – they will often be snapped up before the ship has set sail – then they head for the spa and beauty salon to grab the limited appointments, such as spa and beauty treatments on 'at sea' days rather than 'in port' days. Seasoned cruisers also stake out prime positions around the pool, as loungers in the shade are like gold dust.

of the islands may look similar, with wooded hills surrounding the harbour and mountains stretching into the interior. But on closer inspection, you will discover that each port, and each island, has its own distinctive flavour.

There is no mistaking the French feel of Pointe-à-Pitre in Guadeloupe, for instance, where ships moor next to the bustling Place de la Victoire, with its cafés, war memorial and colourful market. But just to the north, you'll find Antigua, where memories of Admiral Lord Nelson, an Anglican cathedral and a cricket ground give the island a resolutely British feel.

Whether you want to slap on the sun lotion, read a good book and bask in the sun, dive in the sea to discover pristine coral reefs and shipwrecks, hike through a rainforest, or explore ancient Maya ruins, a Caribbean cruise can give you a taste of all of these things and more. It is also possible to combine one cruise itinerary with another (on the same ship or two different ones) for two weeks' cruising.

Forward planning

To get value for money from shore excursions offered on the ship do your homework and research on the places you want to see beforehand. You may find it cheaper to explore an island or area on your own, or with just a few others by taxi. Take care not to overbook excursions, as a crowded schedule can be punishing on the pocket as well as physically exhausting.

Building Bigger

In recent years, most of the islands have experienced an enormous increase in cruise arrivals. The ships have also got larger. The two largest – Royal Caribbean International's 220,000-ton *Oasis of the Seas* and its sister, *Allure of the Seas*, with a maximum capacity of 6,300 passengers, spend all year in the Caribbean because they are simply too big to be accommodated anywhere else.

The Bay of Castries, St Lucia

Most Caribbean ports of call have done a great deal to upgrade and modernise their cruise terminal facilities as cruise numbers rise and larger ships appear. Visitors can normally expect an array of shops, bars and restaurants on shore. But it would be a mistake not to take a look at what is beyond and explore.

In Port

With a few exceptions, cruise ships moor close to the centre of the major Caribbean ports. In the smaller islands it is normally only a brief walk or taxi ride from ship to town. This means you can quickly be at the heart of things.

Usually in the capital or main town, the port would have seen the height of the sugar trade. As a result, they are full of historic interest, revealing ancient warehouses, colonnaded arcades and imposing buildings as well as the traditional fortifications.

WHERE TO GO

The Caribbean has it all: sheltered coves; cooling trade winds; lush rainforests and exotic wildlife – paradise. From the glitzy ships to islands as different as Barbados and St-Barthélemy, this guide aims to cover the popular ports of call, including places not considered part of the region, such as the Bahamas, Mexico and Central America, but which are often found on Caribbean cruise itineraries.

SAILING OUT OF AMERICA

The majority of cruises to the Caribbean begin at US ports and most of those are in Florida, particularly for the western and eastern cruise routes. But since 11th September 2001, when many Americans were put off flying, cruises have been departing from a wider range of ports, notably New Orleans, in Louisiana, and Galveston and Houston in Texas. For southern Caribbean cruises, more routes start from Barbados and San Juan in Puerto Rico so that itineraries can take in more islands.

If you are going on a cruise and have extra time, you can have a land-based holiday first or stay on after disembarking.

Miami

The main gateway to the Caribbean and its islands, Miami has the largest cruise passenger port in the world, with over 3 million passengers passing through it every year. Major cruise lines such as Carnival Cruise Lines, Norwegian Cruise Line (NCL) and Royal Caribbean International (RCI) depart from the terminal here.

The city's intoxicating ambience is a draw, and many like

Small ship adventures with the Blount cruise line

USA

Location: **Miami** is on the southeastern Florida coast; **Fort Lauderdale** is about 35km (23 miles) north of Miami; **Port Canaveral** is at the northern end of Florida's Space Coast, 56km (35 miles) east of Orlando; **Tampa** is on Florida's east coast 120km (75 miles) southeast of Orlando; and **Key West** is at the very end of the Florida Keys, the islands off the tip of Florida, 260km (159 miles) from Miami. **New Orleans** is on the Mississippi Delta by the Gulf of Mexico. The two main ports for Texas are the city of **Houston** and the island of **Galveston** 80km (50 miles) to the south, also on the Gulf coast.

Time zones: UTC/GMT -4 (Florida); UTC/GMT -5 (New Orleans, Texas).

Population: 2.1 million (Greater Miami); 600,000 (Miami City); 150,000 (Fort Lauderdale); 300,000 (Tampa); 25,500 (Key West); 484,674 (New Orleans); 1.95 million (Houston); 57,247 (Galveston).

Language: English (and Spanish in Miami).

Money matters: The US dollar ($) is divided into 100 cents (¢). Credit cards are accepted and there are plenty of ATMs (cashpoints). Travellers from outside the US should bring US$ travellers' cheques.

Telephone & Internet: Payphones are everywhere and take a quarter (25¢) coin. Buy a phone card (from visitor centres and shops) to call long distance. To call long distance within the US, dial 1+area code+local number; or to call overseas you must dial 011+country code+area code+local number.

Area codes: 305 (Miami and Key West); 954 (Fort Lauderdale); 321 (Port Canaveral); 813 (Tampa); 504 (New Orleans); 713, 281 and 282 (Houston); 409 (Galveston).

Internet cafés are plentiful too; ask at the tourist office in the port.

Calendar highlights: Halloween: Miami, Tampa, New Orleans. Miami: Carnival (Feb/Mar), St Patrick's Day (Mar); Fort Lauderdale: Las Olas Arts Festival (Mar), Seafood Festival (April); Cape Canaveral: Warbird Air Show (Mar), Space Coast State Fair (Nov); New Orleans: Mardi Gras (Feb/Mar); Tampa: Gasparilla Pirate Festival (Feb).

to include a few days or a week here in their holiday plans.

In southeast Florida, Greater Miami sprawls over 5,180 sq km (2,000 sq miles) in Dade County and is home to more than 2 million people, including immigrants from Latin America and the Caribbean, particularly from Cuba.

The **Port of Miami** (tel: 305-371 7678), on Dodge Island, 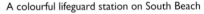 straddles Biscayne Bay between the city and Miami Beach. A top-class facility, the port has excellent security, plenty of car parking and check-in counters that can issue boarding passes for return flights home. **Miami International Airport**, only 13km (8 miles) away, has shuttle buses specifically for cruise passengers and a constant supply of taxis.

South Beach

Even if you just have a few hours to spare in Miami, a trip to **South Beach**, a few miles east of the port, should be a priority.

A colourful lifeguard station on South Beach

The vibrant, flamboyant southern neighbourhood of **Miami Beach** is where everyone goes to see and be seen and, within 2.5 sq km (1 sq mile), it contains more than 800 well-preserved art deco buildings in the **Art Deco National Historic District**.

Start off on Ocean Drive, Florida's most famous street, at the **Art Deco Welcome Center** (daily 10am–6pm; tel: 305-672 2014; www.mdpl.org) and either sign up for a walking tour or pick up a free map along with any other information and souvenirs. The wonderful pastel 1930s' buildings are testament to the drive of the Miami Design Preservation League (MDPL), who fought off developers in the late 1970s.

Inside are murals of flamingos and etched glass windows. Even the lifeguard stations on the beach opposite are in pink art deco designs.

A cosmopolitan mix of colourful characters completes the scene at South Beach, and you can watch them go by from one of the many cafés and restaurants along the rather kitsch seafront, or join them in the nightclubs. Remember that to enter a bar or club you must have ID to prove you are 21 years old or over.

Away from the beach, the scene continues to buzz in the pedestrian-only **Lincoln Road Mall** between 16th and 17th streets. Here the art world flourishes, with the **Art Center South Florida** (Mon–Wed 11am–10pm, Thur–Sun 11am–11pm) displaying the work of more than 100 artists, along with open studios where you can watch them at work.

Retail therapy

Shopaholics can have a field day in Florida, especially if kitsch is your bag, and there are plenty of shops selling designer clothes at factory prices.

For a different kind of architecture, and also under the auspices of the MDPL, go to **Espanola Way**, just south of 15th Street. This eye-catching collection of bright pink Moorish arcades and hidden courtyards was built in Mediterranean Revival style in the 1920s and now houses a selection of galleries, cafés and shops. It was also the setting for many scenes of the latter-day TV series *Miami Vice*.

Downtown Miami

Driving west from South Beach, the view of downtown offers a big-city skyscraper skyline. Bilingual and multicultural but with an Hispanic heart, the centre of Miami is closer to the port and has a few interesting places to see. First on the horizon is the tiered **Bank of America Tower** on SE 2nd Street, built by architect I.M. Pei in 1983 as one of the tallest office skyscrapers south of New York. Another distinctive building is the Spanish-style, peach-coloured **Freedom Tower**, which was originally built as offices for the *Miami News* in 1925 and then became the reception centre for Cubans fleeing Fidel Castro's 1959 revolution.

Freedom Tower is a symbol of liberty for Cubans

Opposite the edifice, on the waterfront, is **Bayside Marketplace**, the bustling outdoor shopping mall (Mon–Thur 10am–10pm, Fri–Sat 10am–11pm, Sun 11am–9pm). As well as shops in the waterside complex, there are bars and restaurants, and often live entertainment in the forecourt. You can also take a boat trip from here.

Tabaqueros hard at work

There are two notable museums in the **Miami-Dade Cultural Center** (Tue–Fri 10am–5pm, Sat–Sun noon–5pm; charge; tel: 305-375 3000), on West Flagler Street, – the **Historical Museum of Southern Florida**, which provides a good background to the city's colourful history, and the popular **Miami Art Museum**, with a cosmopolitan mix of permanent and visiting exhibits.

Little Havana

Travelling southward along the coast, you come to **Calle Ocho** (SW 8th Street), which takes you into the heart of **Little Havana**, the core of the Cuban community where the aroma of rich Cuban coffee fills the air. Calle Ocho is lined with interesting shops, Caribbean-style fruit stands and factories where specialists *(tabaqueros)* roll cigars by hand. The **Bay of Pigs Monument**, at the top of Cuban Memorial Boulevard, commemorates those who lost their lives in the failed invasion of Cuba in 1961. Elderly Cubans gather to play dominoes and talk about the lives they left behind in **Domino Park**, and **Woodlawn Park Cemetery** is where three former presidents of Cuba are buried.

A short distance southwest in the smart neighbourhood of **Coral Gables**, full of magnificent homes, you can take a tour of the lavish historic **Biltmore Hotel** (tel: 1-800 915 1926, www.biltmorehotel.com) where the likes of Judy Garland and Al Capone have stayed. Johnny Weissmuller, aka Tarzan, used to be a swimming instructor here and set a world swimming record in the hotel's pool in the 1930s.

Returning to the port via the one-time artists' colony of upmarket **Coconut Grove**, make time to visit the **Vizcaya Museum and Gardens** (Wed–Mon 9.30am–4.30pm; charge; tel: 305-250 9133; www.vizcayamuseum.com), an Italian Renaissance-style palace with large formal gardens. Built in 1916, the villa is full of period furniture and valuable European antiques.

A Trip to the Everglades

The **Everglades National Park** (tel: 305-242 7700; www. nps.gov/ever) is just an hour or two away from Miami. Many cruise lines offer an excursion here at the end of a cruise. Around 350 varieties of birds, 500 kinds of fish, 55 species of reptile, including crocodiles and alligators, and 40 mammal species live in the Everglades. It even has 45 indigenous species of plants that are found nowhere else on earth. You can spot some of them by walking along the numerous boardwalk trails or taking an airboat ride that skims over the swampland.

Everglades National Park

The **Ernest F. Coe Visitor Center** (daily 8am–5pm) is at the park's main entrance on SR 9336, providing maps and brochures, as well as informative displays on various aspects of the park. A word of warning: beware the voracious mosquitoes; pack plenty of insect repellent.

South Florida mall

Make sure you visit the Sawgrass Mills Factory Outlet Mall (12801 W. Sunrise Boulevard; tel: 954-846 2300; Mon–Sat 10am–9.30pm, Sun 11am–8pm), the largest factory outlet mall in the US.

Fort Lauderdale

Ships that sail from Fort Lauderdale dock at the ultra-modern **Port Everglades** (tel: 954-523 3404) in the southern part of the city. About 35km (23 miles) north of Miami, it is the second busiest cruise port in the world, but is far less congested than Port of Miami. Equipped with plenty of parking spaces, taxis, baggage handlers and comfortable waiting areas, it is just 3km (2 miles) from the **Fort Lauderdale/Hollywood International Airport**.

Venice of America

It is hard to believe that less than a hundred years ago, Fort Lauderdale was a massive mangrove swamp stretching down to the coast. The wooden fort that gave the city its name, built in the Seminole Wars in the 1850s, had long since rotted away. The famous white sandy beaches still remain, stretching for 35km (23 miles) from Hollywood in the south to Deerfield Beach in the north.

A 'wave wall' and walkway edge the 11km (7 miles) of beachfront in the city, making it a perfect place for a stroll, bike ride or a jog, with plenty of cafés, restaurants and shops to stop off at along the way.

The mangrove swamp was transformed into building land by using the same technique that was applied to create Venice in Italy – dredging up a series of parallel canals and using the fill to create long peninsulas between them – hence its nickname, Venice of America. Today Fort Lauderdale has 560km (350 miles) of navigable waterways, flanked by beautiful homes; it is a mecca for water sports enthusiasts and yachties.

Las Olas Boulevard

A free hop-on hop-off shuttle links the beach with downtown, and the city's cosmopolitan character, committed to the good life, can be witnessed along **Las Olas Boulevard**. A red-brick street, lined with old-fashioned gaslights, Las Olas offers visitors horse-drawn carriage rides, outdoor cafés, antiques shops and art galleries.

Towards the western end, a network of palm-lined footpaths and mini parks, called the **Riverwalk**, takes you past several historic sites on the banks of the New River. **Las Olas Riverfront** (daily 10am–11pm) is a modern and meandering outdoor complex filled with restaurants, art galleries, boutiques and bars.

Fort Lauderdale colourful coastline

City Museums

Not far from Las Olas Boulevard are several attractions. Housed in a rustic 1905 inn, the **Old Fort Lauderdale Village and Museum** (Tue–Fri 11am–5pm, Sat–Sun noon–5pm; charge; tel: 954-463 4431) contains exhibits on the area's history, including Indian artefacts, historic photos and fine antiques.

Bonnet House (Tue–Sat 10am–4pm, Sun noon–4pm; charge; tel: 954-563 5393; www.bonnethouse.org) is the plantation-style winter home of the late art collector Frederick Bartlett and his wife Evelyn, who were both artists. It is a grand estate filled with unusual art and artefacts from around the world. The **Museum of Discovery and Science** (Mon–Sat 10am–5pm, Sun noon–6pm; charge; tel: 954-467 6637; www.mods.org) is the largest science museum in South Florida and offers educational hands-on exhibits for children as well as an indoor citrus grove.

Closer to the port, if you have not had your fill of being waterborne, you may enjoy the intimate atmosphere of a 3-hour trip aboard the riverboat *Jungle Queen* (tel: 954-462 5596). This old-fashioned vessel will take you from the Bahia Mar Yacht Center along the New River so that you can see the riverside homes of some of the city's millionaires.

Great Gravity Clock, Museum of Discovery and Science

South of Fort Lauderdale is **Hollywood**, which has no connection with Tinseltown in California, but it does have a large entertainment complex of restaurants, bars and shops called **Oceanwalk** and a wonderful oceanfront boardwalk. West and inland you can visit the **Seminole Indian Native Village** (tel: 954-797 5551) and take in an alligator wrestling show.

If you have time, it is worth visiting the **Loxahatchee National Wildlife Refuge** (daily, daylight hours; charge; tel: 561-734 8303), at the most northerly part of the

Everglades. There are walking trails and you can see a variety of birds in their wetland habitat. To reach the refuge head north to Delray Beach and then travel 16km (10 miles) inland.

Port Canaveral

Further north along the Atlantic coast of Florida, beyond Miami and Fort Lauderdale, **Port Canaveral** (tel: 321-783 7831; www.

All aboard the *Jungle Queen* for a New River tour

portcanaveral.org) is a smaller port that caters mostly to the three-, four- and seven-day Caribbean cruise market. Although it may not be as busy as the others, it is still a top-class port with some ultra-modern terminals. This is the base for Disney Cruise Line, which has its own dedicated cruise terminal built to its *Disney Magic* specifications – a second-level 1,200-sq metres (13,000-sq ft) terrace is etched with a map of Florida and the Bahamas. Royal Caribbean and Carnival ships, among others, also depart from this port.

The port has quite a few attractions of its own, you can choose between its three parks or bike along the dedicated 2.5km (1½-mile) trail. There are also deep-sea fishing facilities and several charter companies (www.fishingspacecoast. org) operate half-day or full-day trips for visitors from here. At the restaurants and cafés in **The Cove** leisure area on the waterfront, you can sample the day's catch, cooked straight off the boats, and get some shopping done, too.

Port Canaveral is just 45 minutes away from both **Orlando International Airport** 72km (45 miles) to the west and **Melbourne International Airport** 40km (25 miles) to the south.

Orlando Theme Parks

It's a straight road – the Beeline Expressway – west to **Orlando** and its plethora of theme parks and attractions. Four of the main ones are part of Walt Disney's empire with another two belonging to Universal Studios, so if you like that sort of thing it's worth considering a cruise plus a week or so in Orlando. Cruises departing from here often offer pre- or post-cruise packages to Walt Disney World and other central Florida attractions.

Kennedy Space Center

Stopping for a while at Port Canaveral gives you the opportunity to visit **Kennedy Space Center** (daily 9am–5.30pm, closed some launch days; charge; tel: 321-449 4444 or 888-838-8915). You will need at least a day to tour NASA's launch and landing facilities, try out the rocket simulators, explore a life-size replica of a space shuttle and meet an astronaut – you can have lunch with one for an extra fee. Outside the centre is the **Astronaut Hall of Fame** (daily 9am–8pm; charge, either separate or with the Kennedy Space Center Pass). The potential closure of the manned space shuttle program in 2012 may change the scope of the site's themed programming, but is highly unlikely to disrupt its tourist attraction.

The nearby **Merritt Island National Wildlife Refuge** (daily, daylight hours, tel: 321-861 0667), which sprawls over 57,000 hectares (140,000 acres), is also owned by NASA, as is the **Canaveral National Seashore** (daily 6am–6pm, extended summer hours). The salt marshes of the Refuge are home to hundreds of species of water

Good buys

Main Street Titusville, Olde Cocoa Village and downtown Melbourne offer the best souvenir and knick-knack shops, while the beach shop, Ron Jon Surf Shop claims to sell 'everything under the sun'.

birds, alligators, the threatened manatee and loggerhead turtles. The Seashore is a protected barrier island beach park with sand dunes and a network of marked canoe trails through a lagoon, where you can spot egrets, ibis, cranes, spoonbills, terns and herons.

Tampa

Almost opposite Cape Canaveral on Florida's Gulf Coast lies **Tampa**, a small city by US standards. Its 12-hectare (30-acre) **Garrison Seaport Cruise Terminal** (tel: 813-905 5131) at the Port of Tampa has car parking and baggage handling facilities, and is only 24km (15

Astronaut gear on display at
Kennedy Space Center

miles) from Tampa International Airport. The city is becoming popular as a turnaround port and most of the main cruise operators berth ships here, mainly sailing to Mexico and the islands of the Western Caribbean.

With a few hours to spare, you will find plenty to do in the terminal's massive **Channelside** complex, which has shops full of designer clothes and cigars, plus bars and cinemas, and you won't want to miss a visit to the state-of-the-art **Florida Aquarium** (daily 9.30am–5pm; charge; tel: 813-273 4000), considered to be one of the best in the US. It features more than 4,000 varieties of fish including sharks and stingrays.

The Tampa skyline is as vibrant as the city's nightlife

Theme Park Thrills

If you are staying in Tampa for a few days, you can experience an Orlando-style theme park at **Busch Gardens** (daily 10am–6pm, extended hours in summer and holidays; charge; tel: 813-987 5000; www.buschgardens.com). More akin to an African safari theme park, with a wide range of wild animals roaming free, it offers some world-class thrilling rides that are guaranteed to scramble your brains. Arrive prepared to get wet on some of the rides and allow a day to get the best out of a visit.

Orlando *(see page 32)*, with its famous theme parks, is only 120km (75 miles) away and worth a day trip, but make sure you plan carefully before you go, to make the most of it.

Downtown Tampa

The majestic minarets of the 19th-century Tampa Bay Hotel look out of place on the city's modern skyline. Today, the former hotel, built by a Florida railway magnate and now part of the University of Tampa campus, is home to the **Henry B. Plant Museum** (Tue–Sat 10am–5pm, Sun noon–5pm; charge; tel: 813-254 1891), which contains some of its original furniture and valuable artefacts. Tours are available.

Established in 1886 by a Cuban cigar factory owner, **Ybor City** is an historic neighbourhood of old buildings, colourful Spanish-style tiles and wrought-iron gates. The **Ybor City State Museum** (1818 East 9th Avenue; daily 9am–5pm; tel: 813-247 6323) does a good job of explaining the history of the cigar-manufacturing community.

New Orleans

This throbbing city of jazz and gumbo, in Louisiana on the Mississippi River, is slowly being restored to its former glory after the devastation of Hurricane Katrina. The **Port of New Orleans** (www.portno.com) operates **Julia Street Cruise Terminals** 1 and 2 and the newer **Erato Street Terminal** alongside with lots of car parking space.

New Orleans is a great place in which to spend a few extra days, offering world-famous nightlife and riverboat trips. Within walking distance of the terminal lies the atmospheric **French Quarter**, (virtually untouched by the hurricane) here there is no shortage of walking or taxi tours to choose from. Royal Street and Bourbon Street are the most colourful, especially at Mardi Gras, which marks the last day before the beginning of Lent.

Jackson Square is the ideal place to start a tour, on foot or by horse-drawn carriage. Most tours take in the **New Orleans Historic**

Amusement park

Busch Gardens has one of the best collections of rollercoasters in Florida. If you are visiting the park, be sure to collect a map at the entrance because the layout can be confusing.

Voodoo Museum (724 Dumaine Street; daily 10am–6pm; charge; www. voodoomuseum.com) and a typical Creole meal at **Brennan's Restaurant** (417 Royal Street, tel: 504-525 9711; www.brennansneworleans.com). Also worth a stop is the **Museé Conti Wax Museum** (917 Rue Conti; Mon, Fri, Sat 10am–4pm; charge; www.neworleanswax museum.com), featuring dioramas depicting important people and events in Louisiana's history.

Galveston

 An island town in Texas, the **Port of Galveston** (www.port ofgalveston.com) is home port to Carnival Conquest, Carnival Conquest and Royal Caribbean's Voyager of the Seas, covering the Mexican coast to Belize, as well as Jamaica and the Cayman Islands.

Close to the terminal is **The Strand**, a renovated warehouse district full of shops and restaurants, and reminiscent of New Orleans' Bourbon Street, and like that colourful city, Galveston makes a big thing of Mardi Gras. If you can't be there for the pre-Lenten carnival, pop into the **Mardi Gras Museum** (23rd Street and Strand; Mon–Fri 10am–8pm, Sat

US Home Ports

Since the 2001 terrorist attacks in the US, the ports of New Orleans, Galveston and Houston have grown in popularity as embarkation points for cruises to the Western Caribbean, Belize, Honduras, the Cayman Islands and Mexico's Yucatán Peninsula. This is because many Americans prefer not to fly and these ports along the Gulf Coast, all with good road and rail links to the rest of the country, serve a far-reaching area – a radius of 800km (500 miles) has a catchment of 47 million would-be cruise ship passengers. The major cruise lines – mainly Carnival, Royal Caribbean and NCL – have ships based at these ports.

10am–10pm, Sun 10am–6pm; free; tel: 409-763 1133), which is devoted to the subject of exhibiting historic costumes, photographs and other memorabilia. At the **Texas Seaport Museum** (daily 10am–5pm; charge; tel: 409-763 1877) at Pier 21, you can explore a restored, 19th-century square-rigged tall ship, *Elissa*. Alongside is the **Pier 21 Theater**, which shows a powerful documentary with dramatic sound effects of the ferocious Great Storm in 1900, in which the town of Galveston was flattened by the sea and thousands of residents died.

Experience New Orleans' world-famous nightlife

Houston

About 80km (50 miles) north of Galveston, the **Port of Houston** (tel: 713-670 2400; www.portofhouston.com) flourished at the expense of its hurricane-blown neighbour. A canal turned the city into an inland port, which is one of the three busiest in the US. A veritable forest of skyscrapers knitted together by motorways, the city is home to NASA's **Space Center**, and has a culture of eccentricity.

Key West

Key West is literally at the end of the road – the US1, in fact, that connects the arc of islands called the Florida Keys with the mainland. The town is often the first port of call on a

Western Caribbean cruise and has a flamboyant, offbeat personality of its own. As the Old Town is so small, you can wander around it easily and take in the gingerbread architecture, literary legacies and other historic landmarks.

The **Port of Key West** (tel: 305-293 8309) is perfectly positioned by **Mallory Square**, right in the middle of **Old Town**, and each year around 700,000 cruise passengers disembark here and at the Mole Pier a little further away. Every evening there's a **Sunset Celebration**, when jugglers, mime artists, musicians, dancers and animal tamers come into the square and put on a free show.

Shipwrecks

For a classic tour of Key West visitors can either take the historic **Conch Tour Train** (daily 9am–4.30pm; charge), which has been giving narrated rides through the town since 1958, or the newer **Old Town Trolley**; both depart from Mallory

Hemingway's Home

The **Ernest Hemingway Home and Museum** (daily 9am–5pm; charge; tel: 305-294 1575; www.hemingwayhome.com) on Whitehead Street, is where literary legend 'Papa' Hemingway lived with his second wife Pauline and their two sons from 1931 to 1939 when they divorced. He then moved to Cuba and she stayed on in the beautiful 19th-century Spanish colonial house until her death in 1951. Hemingway would use it as a stopover base until he died in 1961. He used to write in the cool of the mornings in his studio by the swimming pool – the first to be built in Key West – and he wove his many characterful local friends into his stories. His novel *To Have And Have Not* is a fine example of this. Perfectly preserved, the house is full of his antique furniture, art, old books and hunting trophies, giving the visitor a clear view into his life during his time there.

Square every 20 or 30 minutes. However, if you prefer to see the sights under your own steam, you can hire a bike from several outlets.

Mallory Square and harbour

Key West's past is built on the bounty of the many ships that were wrecked off the island. The late diving pioneer Mel Fisher found heaps of treasure on the sea bed; you can see it at the **Mel Fisher Maritime Heritage Society and Museum** (200 Greene Street; Mon–Fri 8.30am–5pm, Sat–Sun 9.30am–5pm; charge; tel: 305-294 2633).

The **Little White House** (111 Front Street; daily 9am–5pm; charge; tel: 305-294 9911), which chronicles the many holidays that US President Harry S. Truman took here during the 1940s, is another popular attraction.

On Duval Street

Duval Street bisects the Old Town and is lined with shops and restaurants such as pop star Jimmy Buffet's Margaritaville Café. Occupying the oldest house in Key West at no.322 is the **Wreckers Museum** (daily 10am–4pm; charge; tel: 305-294 9502) containing antiques and artefacts that tell the story of the notorious pirates who raided ships off this coast during the 1700s. The oddest attraction, though, is **Ripley's Believe It Or Not! Museum** (daily 9.30am–7pm; charge; tel: 305-293 9939) with a curious collection of diving antiques and authentic shrunken heads. Sloppy Joe's, one of Hemingway's favourite bars, is within staggering distance of his former home *(see page 38)*. Another of his watering holes, Captain Tony's, is close by.

Mexico

Cozumel, **Playa del Carmen** and **Costa Maya**

Location: The Yucatán is a huge, low-lying peninsula jutting out into the Gulf of Mexico in the Caribbean. Ports of entry include **Cozumel**, an island off the northeastern coast; **Playa del Carmen**, a purpose-built resort on the mainland, 19km (12 miles) across the sea from Cozumel; and **Puerto Costa Maya** about 225km (140 miles) further south along the coast of the Yucatán.

Time zone: UTC/GMT -5.

Population: 107 million (all Mexico).

Language: Spanish and local dialects.

Money matters: The unit of currency is the Mexican peso. Travellers' cheques in US dollars are the best way of bringing money in. Major credit cards are widely accepted in tourist areas but for public markets, restaurants and small shops you will need cash. Banks are open Mon–Fri 9am–4.30pm.

Telephone & Internet: The country code is +52, area code 987 (Cozumel); 984 (Playa del Carmen), 998 (Costa Maya). Payphones are available, for which you need a phone card (sold on newsstands). There are internet cafés in both Playa del Carmen and Cozumel, including one at 798 Avenue Rafael E. Melgar.

Beaches: On Cozumel, Playa del Sol or San Francisco Beach to the south or Playa Azul to the north have soft sand and facilities. Playa del Carmen is one long beach; the northern end is quieter. There is a good beach at Majahual next to Puerto Costa Maya.

Shopping: In Cancun, a 90-minute bus ride north of Playa del Carmen.

Outdoor activities: Watersports, snorkelling, boating, fishing, trips to the nearby antiquities.

Calendar highlights: Equinox Seasonal Event at Chichén Itzá (21 Mar/21 Sept) – a snake-shaped shadow appears on El Castillo pyramid; Cozumel: Carnival (Feb/Mar); San Miguel Arcangel Fiesta (Sept).

MEXICO & CENTRAL AMERICA

Magical ancient Maya ruins, magnificent waterfalls, a spectacular barrier reef, stunning talcum powder beaches, majestic mountains, tropical rainforests, exotic gardens and people with strong national identities all add up to a fascinating and rich cruising experience along the far-reaching Caribbean coastline of Mexico and Central America.

Western Shores cruises vary, depending on the size of the ship, and change annually. Most companies offer three- to five-day itineraries, but often cruises to this region last for 10–14 days, either stopping at all the ports of call or a select few. The ports are all efficiently run, with modern amenities.

As a rule, after leaving the US, cruises aim for Mexico's **Yucatán Peninsula** just 800km (500 miles) from the Florida coast. Reaching out into the Gulf of Mexico and the

The Pyramid of Kukulcán (El Castillo) at Chichén Itzá

Beautiful beaches

Playa San Francisco, in the southwest, is a beautiful 5km (3-mile) beach offering water sports and restaurants. Playa Bonita is one of the most secluded beaches on Cozumel.

Caribbean Sea, the peninsula's popularity stems from the wealth of archaeological treasures left by the ancient Maya civilization thousands of years ago.

Cozumel

A favourite port of call is **Cozumel**, Mexico's largest island at 48km (30 miles) long and 16km (10 miles) at its widest point. Until recently only a handful of ships a week called here, but it now draws so many that some have to tender passengers to land, usually into **San Miguel**. Those lucky enough to dock do so at the **International Pier** or **Puerto Maya Pier**. Just a few miles from town, both piers are modern facilities with information booths, international phone access and plenty of taxis and rental cars.

Across from the pier is the **Plaza del Sol**, the main town square where locals and tourists gather. The nearby seaside promenade, the **Malecón**, is jammed with craft and souvenir shops, as is the busy **Rafael Melgar Avenue**.

Also on Melgar is the **Museo de la Isla de Cozumel** (Cozumel Island Museum; daily 9am–5pm; charge; tel: 987-872 1434), a former 1930s luxury hotel that now contains exhibits on pre-Columbian and colonial history, maritime artefacts, coral-reef topography and displays on indigenous endangered animals. Guided tours of the museum are in English and Spanish.

For a wonderful insight into the magical world of the reefs offshore, without getting wet, you will find **Atlantis Submarine Tours** (Mon–Sat 10am, 11am, noon; tel: 987-872 5671; www.cozumel-tours.com) in front of the Casa del Mar Hotel, about 3km (2 miles) south of San Miguel.

A popular excursion from Cozumel is a long haul to the Maya site of Tulum on the mainland *(see pages 46–7)*. However, if you would rather not venture so far from San Miguel you can visit **El Cedral**, a small collection of Maya ruins where, every May, a colourful fiesta is held to commemorate the first Catholic Mass celebrated in Mexico in 1518.

Closer to the centre of the island, **San Gervasio** (daily 8am–4pm; charge), hidden in the jungle, is another Maya site, which has a sanctuary to Ixchel, the goddess of fertility, medicine and midwifery. However, although both sites are well preserved, they do not come close in comparison with some of the other Maya settlements on the mainland.

Beaches

At the southwestern end of the island is **Playa San Francisco**, a 3-mile (5km) beach dotted with restaurants and water sports operators.

Other good beaches are **Playa del Sol**, **Playa Plancar** and **Playa Bonita**, but the pride and joy of Cozumel is the popular beach at **Parque Nacional Chankanaab** (Chankanaab National Park; daily 8am–5pm; charge;_tel: 987-872 0914). Along with a beautiful soft sand beach, the park contains a land-locked natural pool connected to the sea by an underground tunnel. It also features a lush

Beach at Cozumel

botanical garden with over 800 species of plants, a small natural history museum, and a swim-with-dolphins programme.

Cancún

The resort city of Cancún has only come into being since 1970 when the first hotel was built along a 22km (14-mile) beach. Today high-rise hotels jostle with golf courses, marinas, restaurants and nightclubs to create a holiday mecca. The turquoise sea and fine beaches here are legendary. Although it's not a cruise ship stop you may visit on a shore excursion from Cozumel or Playa del Carmen, for the beach or shopping at the Orlando-style **La Isla Shopping Village** and **Plaza La Fiesta**.

Food stall in Cancún

Playa del Carmen

The Riviera Maya stretches from Cancún in the north of the Yucatán 160km (100 miles) down to Tulum in the south along a coastline of beautiful white sandy beaches. Although tourist development has increased since the 1980s, turning tiny fishing villages into towns, the beaches are mainly still unspoilt and the Mesoamerican reef provides some of the best diving in the world.

Halfway along the Riviera and opposite Cozumel is **Playa del Carmen**, or Playa as it's commonly referred to, which 20 years ago was a small, peaceful fishing village without electricity. Today, it is one of the busiest ports of call in Mexico with a wealth of places to visit and things to do. Amazingly, the town has not developed into a forest of large resort-style hotels but rather retained a laid-back cosmopolitan atmosphere with a European influence. Old clapboard houses line the streets and a beach and café culture pervades.

Swimming in the underground river at Xcaret

The town revolves around **Avenida Cinco** (Fifth Avenue), a vibrant street, running parallel with the beach, full of in-expensive restaurants, bars offering margaritas, internet cafés, and jewellery shops selling silver and crafts.

Cruises stopping off at Playa either drop anchor off the coast and ferry passengers to shore; dock at Cozumel (see page 42) and ferry passengers back over; or they can dock at the **Puerto Calica Cruise Ship Pier**, about 13km (8 miles) south of the town. Excursions usually include a choice of trips to the Maya sites of Xcaret, Tulum (see page 46), Xel-Há, Cobá and sometimes the big one to Chichén Itzá; or shopping and snorkelling in Cancún, a 90-minute bus ride away.

Xcaret

One of the more popular excursions from Playa is to **Xcaret** (daily 8.30am–9.30pm; charge; tel: 988-251 6560; www. xcaret.com), a uniquely designed ecological and archaeo-logical theme park north of the cruise ship terminal. This is the Yucatán's answer to Disney World, Xcaret (pronounced *ish-car-et*) is a stunningly beautiful and thoroughly modern attraction with myriad diversions. While it is very commercialised, Xcaret can provide an entire day's worth of activities and is great fun for children.

Xel-Há

Another ecopark along similar lines is **Xel-Há** (daily 8.30am–6pm; charge; tel: 984-147 6560; www.xelha.com), which is on the way to Tulum. Xel-Há (pronounced *shell-hah*) means 'the place where water was born' in Maya and its main attribute is a large natural inlet where the sea water mixes with fresh river water and is home to an amazing assortment of underwater life. The banks are covered in jungle laced with walking trails, you can hike to a Maya cave and some of the area's *cenotes (see box)*. **Xpu-Há** (daily 8.30am–5.30pm; entrance fee), pronounced *ish-poo-hah*, is another theme park. Both have snorkelling, scuba and other water sports.

Tulum and Cobá

From Cozumel, as in other ports of call in the Yucatán, you can take an excursion over to the mainland to see the Maya ruins that stand on top of a cliff at **Tulum** (daily 7am–6pm). Expensive but worth it, this day-long trip, which involves a lot of travelling, gives you the opportunity to experience the only Maya site overlooking the sea. The main building, the Castillo, which looks like a castle, is thought to have acted as a lighthouse.

Sinkhole snorkel

The world's largest cavern diving and snorkelling complex can be found just south of Xel-Há at Hidden Worlds Cenotes (tours daily every half hour). Even novice snorkellers can enjoy this magical underground system of caves and *cenotes* (sinkholes).

Most of the site is flat and easy to walk around, but there are small buses operating from the main entrance, if you prefer. With miles of beautiful beaches, cafés and a turquoise sea at the bottom of the cliff, the ruins really do present a dramatic sight.

Inland from Tulum lies the vast Maya city of **Cobá** (daily 8am–5pm; charge). Set around a system of small lakes, there are supposed to be some 6,000 buildings here, although only a few have been excavated, including the **Templo de la Iglesia** (Church Pyramid), with unusual rounded corners, and a ball court. The Nohoch

The Maya ruins at Tulum

Mul (meaning large hill) pyramid, at 42 metres (138ft) high, is the tallest structure in the northern Yucatán and from here there are wonderful views.

Chichén Itzá

The most spectacular excursion in this area, however, is a full-day trip to the Maya ruins of **Chichén Itzá** (daily 9am–5pm; charge), about 150 miles (240km) inland from the coast. While it is costly (more than US$200), time consuming and tiring, a trip to Chichén Itzá is the highlight of any Yucatán holiday.

Among the best known ruins in Latin America, the fabled ancient city provides a fascinating picture of Maya life in the

Pyramid of Kukulcán

10th century. Covering four sq miles (10 sq km), the site contains the towering **Pyramid of Kukulkán** which dominates the archaeological site. There are several temples, an observatory, ball courts, steam baths, a sacrificial well and a ceremonial house. Local guides offer excellent tours in English and there is an on-site restaurant for refreshments and an informative museum. In the evening, Chichén Itzá puts on an impressive, spectacular **sound-and-light show**.

The Maya dominated the people here and also the trade of the entire northern Yucatán, but by the end of the 13th century the city had more or less been abandoned due to revolt and inter-tribal battles breaking out.

Costa Maya

The coast stretching southward from Tulum to Belize is known as the **Costa Maya** and in 2001 a port of call, **Puerto Costa Maya**, was opened about 280km (175 miles) south of Playa del Carmen. With a modern and efficiently run terminal, more akin to a holiday resort, the port quickly became a destination on most of the major cruise line itineraries.

Built next to the small coastal settlement of **Majahual** and a lovely palm-lined beach, the port (www.puertocosta maya.com) is laid out like a Maya city and has first-class amenities, swimming pool and bars, plus bazaars and folkloric shows in authentic-looking pavilions. The region is rich in ruins and has an untouched hinterland of tropical forests and mangrove swamps. Excursions include kayaking, snorkelling and diving trips and hikes in the jungle.

The Maya Legacy

The Maya people occupied the Yucatán, Belize, northern Honduras, Guatemala and El Salvador, and from around AD300–900 they developed dynasties forming a loosely connected network of city states and built impressive pyramids for temples. In the Yucatán, settlements grew up next to *cenotes*, sinkholes where fresh water collected. It was always something of a mystery as to how the Maya could have created such an advanced culture in a region where there was no surface water. Then it was discovered that the cenotes were linked and that water flowed between them; instead of the Nile or the Euphrates, the Maya had their underground rivers, which provided a constant supply of water. Life for the Maya came from below, a fact which might explain why the underworld featured so strongly in their beliefs. As at Chichén Itzá, the *cenotes* often doubled as sacred sites.

The Maya are considered by experts to have been the most advanced people of the Americas. They studied the stars and developed complicated calendar systems that rival even the technology of today for precision and complexity. They worshipped time and every aspect of their lives was driven by the calendar, from when to get married to the right time to sow a crop. They wrote in hieroglyphics, mathematically recording their sacred rituals, and were skilled artists and craftsmen, weaving and producing ceramics and jewellery.

No one really knows why the Maya civilization collapsed towards the end of the first millennium. However, the Maya people live on; some have integrated into the modern world, others retain their ancestral beliefs and are preserving their heritage for the world to see.

Kohunlich

A day trip to the early Classic ruins of **Kohunlich** (daily 9am–5pm; charge), named after the large palm trees growing there, is a popular choice. Here you can see the spectacular Temple of Masks, a pyramid with a central stairway flanked by stucco god masks, built around AD500.

In the Temple of Masks at Kohunlich

Some shore excursions may combine a trip to the ruins with a visit to the excellent **Museo de la Cultura Maya** (daily 9am–7pm; charge), in the border town of **Chetumal**, which showcases miniature reconstructed Maya cities under a glass floor.

Virgin Reef

The port is close to one of the last virgin reefs in the region offering world-class snorkelling and diving. The magnificent **Parque Nacional de Chinchorro Submarino** is about 48km (30 miles) long and 14km (9 miles) wide with depths dropping in places to 900 metres (3,000ft). It has more than 30 sunken ships to explore amid a forest of coral.

The **Reserva de la Biósfera Sian Ka'an** (tel: 984-871 2499) is a vast nature preserve, about 80km (50 miles) north of the port. The wetlands, savannah and jungle contain a variety of marine habitats and are havens for flamingos, colourful parrots and more than 300 other bird species, and wild animals. Be warned: the mosquitoes can be fierce so cover up well and wear repellent.

Belize

Bordered by Mexico in the north and Guatemala to the west and south, the tiny, English-speaking country of Belize, is a favourite port of call. It is a paradise for ecotourism, with the world's second largest barrier reef offshore, coral cays, rivers, mountains, vast swathes of rainforest and jungle, savannah and mangrove coasts, and a rich Maya legacy.

While small vessels can drop anchor at Belize's offshore islands further south and at the smaller town of Dangriga, most large cruise ships call at **Belize City**.

For the time being they must anchor offshore, and use tenders to transport passengers for the 20-minute journey to the Tourism Village, which has been specially designed for day cruise-ship passengers. Here you can find plenty of shops, restaurants and taxis and access to land and marine tours. The centre of town is only a five-minute walk.

Ambergris Caye, Belize

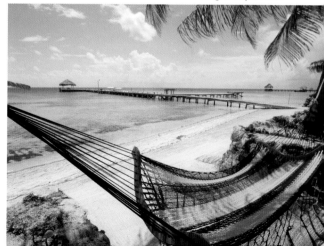

Central America

Belize, **Honduras** and **Costa Rica**

Location: **Belize** (capital Belize City) lies south of Mexico and east of Guatemala. It shares the 300km (185-mile) long Mesoamerican Barrier Reef with the Bay Islands archipelago in Honduras to the south, where **Roatán Island** (main town Coxen Hole) is situated some 48km (30 miles) off the coast. **Costa Rica** (capital San José) lies further south between Nicaragua to the north and Panama.

Time Zone: UTC/GMT -6.

Population: 80,000 (Belize City); 30,000 (Roatán); 4.6 million (Costa Rica).

Language: English (Belize); Spanish, English and local dialects (Roatán); Spanish (Costa Rica).

Money Matters: The Belize dollar (BZ$) has a fixed rate of exchange of BZ$2 to US$1; always check which dollar rate is being quoted when purchasing goods in shops or taking a taxi; bank hours: Mon–Thur 8am–1pm, Fri 8am–4.30pm.

Roatán uses the lempira, although the US dollar is widely accepted in Belize and Honduras. The currency in Costa Rica is the colón. Cash machines can be found in large shopping centres. Private banks are a better option for exchanging foreign currency or travellers' cheques in Costa Rica to avoid two-hour queues in the state banks. Bank hours in Costa Rica: Mon–Fri 9am–3pm.

Telephone & Internet: Country codes: 501 (Belize); 504 (Roatán); 506 (Costa Rica). Phone cards are widely available and there are internet centres in the Tourism Village, Belize City, in J.C. Commercial Center at Coxen Hole on Roatán, and at atec in Puerto Viejo de Limón in Costa Rica.

Beaches: Ambergris Caye (Belize); Tabyana Beach (Roatán); Cahuita National Park and Puerto Viejo (Costa Rica).

Calendar Highlights: Belize: Carnival (Feb/Mar), Baron Bliss Day (Mar); Costa Rica: New Year's Day celebrations last for two days; Puerto Limón Columbus Day Carnival (Oct).

Belize City

Oozing rundown Caribbean atmosphere, Belize City, home to an ethnic mix of 80,000, has some interesting places to see that can be explored on a city tour excursion or by taxi. Towering over the harbour is the **Fort George Lighthouse and Park** with the **Baron Bliss Memorial** beneath it. Baron Bliss was a wealthy British yachtsman who lived here on his yacht for a year until his death in 1926. He left a legacy of US$2 million to the people of Belize from which schools, health clinics, hospitals, museums and libraries still benefit.

Not far from the harbour is **Government House** (Mon–Fri 9am–4pm; charge), a beautiful old colonial mansion. Opposite stands **St John's Cathedral** (daily 7am–3pm), built in 1812 and the oldest Anglican Church in Central America. Just 47km (29 miles) west of the capital is the **Belize Zoo** (daily 9am–4.30pm; charge), where you can see indigenous Belizean animals in their natural surroundings.

Storks and Jaguars

The wildlife reserves in Belize are second to none. The **Crooked Tree Wildlife Sanctuary** (daily 8am–4pm; charge) is north of the city, and its wetlands, punctuated by rivers and lagoons, are the habitat for kites, ospreys, and the rare jabiru stork, the largest bird in the Americas. Look out for the crocodiles and turtles.

Further south, and more accessible from Dangriga, is the **Cockscomb Basin Wildlife Sanctuary and Jaguar Preserve** (daily;

Jaguar Preserve

charge), set in over 415 sq km (160 sq miles) of dense tropical rainforest. There is plenty of bird- and wildlife here, but all you are likely to glimpse of the shy, nocturnal jaguar is a pawprint.

Ruins and Reefs

Apart from the Maya archaeological sites of **Xuanantunich**, near the Guatemalan border – known for its pyramid, El Castillo – and also **Altun Ha**, north of Belize City, you can take a boat trip along the New River to **Lamanai**, an ancient Maya ceremonial centre hidden in the jungle. Visitors can also go on a river ride through a series of caves on an inner tube; or snorkel, dive or kayak around the awe-inspiring coral reef at the **Hol Chan Marine Reserve** on **Ambergris Caye** 56km (35 miles) from the capital. Water taxis are available for those who want to go off on their own to Ambergris Caye and **San Pedro Island**.

Climb the ruins at Lamanai, an ancient Maya ceremonial site

Honduras

The **Islas de la Bahía** (Bay Islands), are a chain of 70 coral islands off the coast of Honduras, that provide an idyllic port of call, with pristine beaches fringed with tall palm trees, lapped by a warm turquoise sea that conceals the magical world of the same coral reef that borders Belize *(see page 54)*. Snorkelling, diving and lazing on the beaches supping chilled drinks are the main activities here.

Roatán

Ships dock at **Roatán**, the largest and most popular island at just 40km (25-miles) long. It is home to 30,000 people, who tend to speak English rather than Spanish. With a jungle interior and

A yellow-naped parrot in the forest

houses on stilts, Roatán is a top dive destination, and at the port there is a wide choice of dive operators. For those not keen to don a tank, there are two glass-bottomed boats that offer a seabird's eye view of the underwater world.

The island has several small hotels and restaurants, and the 3km (2-mile) long, untouched **Camp Bay Beach** at the eastern end is a perfect place to spend a few hours. You can travel around by taxi or by bike, available for hire by the cruise ship pier, or hike along a trail once used by pirates such as Henry Morgan – it is widely believed that there is still buried treasure here waiting to be discovered. Look out for the indigenous red lored parrot, the Lala monkey and the Jesus lizard, which got its name because it can 'walk on water'.

Natural Beauty

The islanders are keen to protect the unspoiled natural beauty of their environment and at **Anthony's Key Resort**, in the Sandy Bay area, the conservationist museum, the **Roatán Institute for Marine Sciences** (Mon–Fri 7am–5pm, Sat–Sun 8am–5pm; charge), has environmentally aware tours and encounters with dolphins. Nearby, at the **Tropical Treasures Bird Park**, you can see the most comprehensive collection of parrots in Central America.

Costa Rica

A dramatically beautiful country, Costa Rica is a peaceful and democratic oasis in a region torn apart by turmoil. With no armed forces to speak of, the Costa Ricans have benefitted from their resources being put into health, education and conservation rather than national defence. As a result, a quarter of the country's natural assets – its tropical rainforests, gushing rivers, active volcanoes, wonderful wildlife and glorious beaches – are protected, providing a popular destination for eco- and adventure tourists alike.

Limón

 Columbus landed here on his final voyage declaring the place a rich coast – *costa rica*. **Limón** is a palm-fringed city with a

---

San Blas Islands

The smaller cruise ships often stop at the San Blas Islands that lie just off the northeast coast of Panama. Here, on these beautiful Caribbean islands without one brick of development, you can witness Kuna Amerindians living the simple Indian lifestyle, according to centuries-old traditions. The San Blas incorporate more than 60 islands supporting a population of about 30,000 Kuna.

They paddle out to the ships in dugout canoes to sell their wares, or tenders bring passengers ashore from the smaller ships. On land, you will experience a real time warp. Most of the Kuna speak only their native language and live in bamboo huts without electricity or running water. Fishing, farming and making *molas* – an intricate, patchwork-type of embroidery – are their livelihood.

mountain backdrop and an atmosphere that is more Afro-Caribbean than Latin American – many residents here speak English. It is a lively but slightly run-down city with a sprinkling of old wooden houses painted in bright pastel colours.

Parque Vargas, in the centre, is lined with dense with tropical trees and plants. Most Western Caribbean

Costa Rica's dense rainforest

cruises stop here and passengers are ferried ashore.

Some cruises offer trips to the busy capital, **San José**, 112km (70 miles) inland. It's a long day but there are some excellent museums, such as the **Museo de Oro** (Gold Museum; Tue–Sat 9.15am–5pm; charge), which documents the gold fever that consumed the conquistadors.

Taste of Adventure

The diversity of the Costa Rican countryside provides visitors with a range of excursions: whitewater rafting trips; biking or kayaking through wildlife refuges, or bird- and turtle-watching, and eco-tours. Some operators offer a trip through the rainforest canopy of **Parque Nacional Braulio Carrillo**, 35 metres (120ft) above ground in the Rainforest Aerial Tram. At the **Parque Nacional Cahuita**, glass-bottomed boats will take you over the coral reef, and hiking trails wind through lush rainforest.

Nearer Limón, about 24km (15 miles) away, is the small and quirky town of **Puerto Viejo de Limón**. An eclectic mix of surfers, Rastafarians, expats and world-weary travellers gather here and the party atmosphere is contagious.

The Bahamas

Location: The Bahamas is an archipelago of over 700 islands that start 97km (60 miles) off the eastern coast of Florida and stretch southeast for 900km (560 miles) to the edge of the Caribbean Sea. Just over 30 of the islands are inhabited and 20 are well developed for tourism with **New Providence Island** and **Grand Bahama** providing the main ports of call.

Time zone: UTC/GMT -4

Population: 341,700

Language: English; Creole

Money matters: The unit of currency is the Bahamian dollar (B$). US dollars and credit cards are widely accepted. Bank hours: Mon–Thur 9.30am–3pm, Fri 9.30am–5pm.

Telephone & Internet: Country code: +242. The telephone system is sophisticated, with high-speed internet access and roaming agreements with many US cellular phone networks. Nassau, the capital, has several internet cafés, including a communications centre at Festival Place, the cruise ship terminal. The internet is available in the Lucayan Harbour Cruise Facility on Grand Bahama Island.

Beaches: Cable Beach in Nassau (New Providence Island) and at the Atlantis Resort on Paradise Island; Paradise Cove and Fortune Beach (Grand Bahama).

Shopping: Bay Street in Nassau is one of the best areas for fine china, crystal and figurines, French perfumes, fine gems and local crafts. Haggle for less expensive items at the Straw Market. Shopping hours: Mon–Sat 9am–5pm.

Outdoor activities: Water sports, submarine rides, golf, horse riding, dolphin encounters, caving and kayaking (Grand Bahama).

Calendar highlights: Heritage Festival (April); Junkanoo (Dec/Jan) Junkanoo in June (Nassau, June); Eleuthera Pineapple Festival (June); Emancipation Day (Aug); All Abaco Sailing Regatta (Sept); One Bahamas Music and Heritage Festival (Nov).

Children of Grand Bahama

THE BAHAMAS

Despite the fact that the Bahamas are in the Atlantic, New Providence Island or Grand Bahama are often among the first ports of call on a Caribbean cruise itinerary, particularly if the cruise departs from any of the eastern Florida ports.

New Providence Island

Nassau, the national capital, on New Providence Island, has one of the biggest ports on most itineraries, with enough docking at Prince George Wharf to accommodate a dozen cruise ships at a time. **Festival Place** includes a communications centre, an internet café and authentic Bahamian arts and crafts. At the **Junkanoo Expo**, located on the wharf, visitors can see the brightly coloured costumes worn for the carnival-style celebrations on Boxing Day and New Year's Day.

Bargain Bahamas

With no sales tax and low tariffs, the Bahamas offer bargain shopping. Some imported goods are priced 30 to 50 percent lower than in the US, but check out what goods cost at home first.

Cruise ship passengers disembark virtually into the centre of this bustling one-time British colonial capital and there is usually plenty of time for a guided walking tour around the historic parts or a ferry trip to nearby **Paradise Island** *(see page 62)* or a flutter at the gambling table in the casinos of the luxurious Atlantis Resort. The dock is a pedestrian zone, so taxis, buses and tours are only available outside the terminal checkpoint.

Nassau

The city of Nassau is situated on the North Shore of New Providence Island, which is roughly 32km (20 miles) in circumference, and 13km (8 miles) wide. Around 180 nautical miles southeast of Miami, Florida, it is home to almost a quarter of a million people. For many, the busy capital is the Bahamas.

There are plenty of ways to get to know Nassau with only a day in port. One of the most popular (and excellent value) is a professionally guided walking tour of the city with a Bahamahost. This is a local guide, trained by the Ministry of Tourism, who can take groups of up to 10 people on one-hour walks around two different areas of historic Nassau.

Either on the tour or exploring on your own, you will see the pretty, 19th-century, colonial buildings of **Parliament Square**, just off Bay Street, housing the government offices. The islands became an English colony in 1629, were briefly ruled by the Spanish in 1782 and eventually gained their independence from Britain in 1973 as the Commonwealth of the Bahamas. Continuing south, you will arrive at the **Supreme Court** building and the pink, octagonal **Nassau**

Public Library, built in 1798. Once a prison, it contains a small collection of Amerindian artefacts.

Parliament Street has some more splendid colonial buildings, most of them dating from the mid-19th century. Further west stand three houses of worship: **St Andrew's Presbyterian Church**, known as The Kirk; the **Trinity Methodist Church**; and **Christ Church Cathedral**, which has a beautiful stained-glass window above the altar.

A horse-drawn surrey departs from Woodes Rogers Walk, at the port entrance, for a 20-minute clatter along Bay Street and around Old Nassau with a Bahamahost-trained guide. Rates are usually negotiable.

Pirates in the Bahamas

In the 17th and 18th centuries pirates and privateers – those with permission from the British Crown to attack ships for their treasure – terrorised the Caribbean and the waters around the Bahamas. And from 1700, they occupied Nassau, creating anarchy and frightening any law-abiding citizen, chasing them off to the smaller islands. The most notorious of them all was Blackbeard (Edward Teach) who made Nassau Fort his home. His story and others are told at the interactive **Pirates of Nassau Museum** (Mon–Sat 9am–6pm,

Nassau Government offices

Bahamian straw baskets can make useful souvenirs

Sun 9am–noon; charge), opposite the cathedral.

On the 10-minute walk back to the ship you will pass the **Straw Market**, selling baskets, dolls, table mats and hats, all made from plaited thatch palm by crafts people living in the city and on the smaller out islands. The original straw market and neighbouring buildings burned down in 2001.

Paradise Island

At Prince George Wharf, you can take a taxi or ferry, either with an organised tour or on your own, to the smart resorts on **Paradise Island** across Nassau Harbour. Once known less glamorously as Hog Island, its expensive pleasures number the huge **Atlantis Resort** and casino; the **Hurricane Hole**, a haven for luxury yachts; the **Yoga Retreat**; a 14th-century **Gothic Cloister**, brought from France and reconstructed stone by stone; the **Versailles Gardens** surrounding the exclusive Ocean Club Hotel; and the 18-hole championship **Ocean Club Golf Course**. There is also a crescent-shaped white beach.

Grand Bahama

Three times the size of New Providence, Grand Bahama sits at the northern end of the Bahamas chain. It lies 105km (65 miles) east of West Palm Beach and 128km (80 miles) northeast of Miami and has a population of just over 50,000. Freeport, the nation's northernmost island, is not as atmospheric as Nassau, having only come into being in the 1960s. However, it makes a good launching pad for an island that has plenty to offer, from limestone caves and exotic gardens to white sandy beaches, nature walks and eco-adventures – and casinos.

The **Lucayan Harbour Cruise Facility** can accommodate the largest ships in the world and the huge multimillion dollar terminals have everything a cruise passenger could need. The port lies to the west of central Freeport and there are plenty of taxis available if you want to explore alone.

Freeport

Although most of the attractions of Grand Bahama lie outside town a little way, there are some things to see and do in **Freeport**. Near the centre, you can visit the **International Bazaar**, a large shopping precinct with a few bargains and a good range of photographic equipment, plus a Colombian Emeralds outlet. To the east of the Bazaar is a straw market, in case you haven't bought a basket yet, while, on the other side, the **Royal Oasis Golf Resort and Casino** has a spectacular freshwater beach pool (open to the public; charge), with slides, a waterfall, swim-up bar and two golf courses.

Port Lucaya buzzes with life around the market place, with straw craft shops, bijou boutiques, plentiful restaurants and live entertainment in Count Basie Square.

Snorkelling in Grand Bahama

Dolphins in Sanctuary Bay

The Dolphin Experience (charge) located at Sanctuary Bay, a 4-hectare (9-acre) lagoon, is just a short ferry ride from the UNEXSO (Underwater Explorers' Society, www.unexso. com) dock at Port Lucaya. A visit to the bay includes a tour of around 2½ hours, during which visitors can enjoy various kinds of fun in-the-water encounters with the dolphins.

Be aware, however, that captive dolphins are not domesticated animals and many have been captured from the wild. Interactions between humans and these potentially dangerous captive animals take place in a confined, artificial environment where dolphins are rewarded with food for performing tricks. Aggressive behaviour towards swimmers by these unpredictable creatures does occur from time to time.

Performing dolphins

Nature trails

At the 40-hectare (100-acre) **Rand Nature Centre** (Mon–Fri 9am–4.30pm; charge), to the north of Freeport, you can follow some interesting nature trails through natural coppice and pine forests, and see a flock of West Indian flamingos. You may also spot a humming bird and the rare olive capped warbler. Run by the Bahamas National Trust, this National Park has well-informed guides who will enthusiastically enlighten you on the ecology of the Bahamian forest. A monthly bird walk is held on the first Saturday of each month. The peak bird-watching season is from October to May.

The **Garden of the Groves** (daily 9am–5pm; daily guided tours 11am, 2pm; charge) to the east of Freeport and Port Lucaya, is a wondrous botanical garden with cascading waterfalls, and The garden is named after Georgette and Wallace Groves, who created this lovely spot and Groves also founded the Grand Bahama Port authority.

The garden has over 10,000 plants and native birds such as the Cuban emerald and the Greater Antillean bullfinch can be spotted amongst the lush vegetation.

Underwater caves

At the **Lucayan National Park** (daily 9am–4pm; charge), about 21km (13 miles) east of the Garden of the Groves, you can explore the caves that form one of the longest charted underwater cave systems in the world. Accompanied by knowledgeable guides, you can enter the caves by sea or by land and see where artefacts and bones relating to the island's first inhabitants have been discovered.

The 16-hectare (40-acre) park has trails through pine forests rich in tropical vegetation, including orchids. Mangrove lagoons brim with birdlife.

If you don't have much time in port, you can choose to join an organised snorkelling or kayaking trip; or just chill out at a beach party on the beautiful Lucayan Beach or Taino Beach, about 4km (2 miles) from the port.

The Western Caribbean

Cuba, Grand Cayman, Jamaica, Dominican Republic and **Puerto Rico** (Greater Antilles)

Location: The Republic of **Cuba** (capital Havana) is more than 1,250km (775 miles) long and 190km (118 miles) wide, and 150km (93 miles) south of Miami. **Grand Cayman** (George Town), part of the Cayman Islands, lies south of Cuba and northwest of Jamaica. **Jamaica** (Kingston) lies 145km (90 miles) south of Cuba and 160km (100 miles) west of Haiti. The **Dominican Republic** (Santo Domingo) occupies the eastern part of the island of Hispaniola, shared with Haiti, 97km (60 miles) east of Cuba. **Puerto Rico** (San Juan) lies just 87km (54 miles) east of the Dominican Republic.

Time zones: UTC/GMT -4 (Puerto Rico); utc/gmt -5 (Cuba, Dominican Republic, Grand Cayman, Jamaica).

Population: 11.2 million (Cuba); 2.7 million (Jamaica); 10.1 million (Dominican Republic); 4.0 million (Puerto Rico); 51,000 (Grand Cayman).

Language: Spanish (Cuba and Dominican Republic); English/patois (Jamaica); Spanish/English (Puerto Rico); English (Grand Cayman).

Money matters: Cuba: the Cuban peso (CUP$), is used by local people, the Cuban convertible peso (CUC$) is used by tourists; Grand Cayman: Cayman Islands dollar (CI$); Jamaica: Jamaican dollar (J$); Dominican Republic: the peso (RD$); Puerto Rico: US$. Main credit cards are accepted everywhere, except American ones in Cuba; US dollars are accepted in almost all tourist areas (but not Cuba), use small denominations. In shops change is given in local currency.

Telephone & Internet: Country codes: +53 (Cuba); +876 (Jamaica); +345 (Cayman Islands); +809 (Dominican Republic); +787 (Puerto Rico). In Cuba internet facilities are limited, although hotels usually have access. Internet access is available elsewhere especially in the larger hotels.

Calendar highlights: Carnivals: Havana (July), Jamaica (Mar/Apr); Grand Cayman: Pirates' Week (Oct); San Juan: Bautista Night (June).

Street scene, Havana Cuba

THE WESTERN CARIBBEAN

For the purposes of this book, the Western Caribbean comprises the larger islands of Cuba, Jamaica, Dominican Republic and Puerto Rico, with tiny Grand Cayman as one of the main ports of call on western itineraries and San Juan in Puerto Rico a homeport for ships heading south. Although these islands are all close to each other in geographical terms, culturally they are worlds apart.

Cuba

As Cuba, the largest of all the Caribbean islands, has been growing in popularity as a holiday destination, more and more cruise lines are including a stop in Havana on their itineraries. However, there are still major restrictions in place for US citizens, due to the 1961 US embargo. In a nutshell, they cannot travel directly from America to Cuba, nor can they spend any money here. No US-owned cruise line can do business in Cuba and ships from other countries wanting to stop here cannot start their voyage from an American port. Some believe that Americans travelling with non-US companies can legally stop at Havana on a free Cuban 'in transit' visa for up to 48 hours as long as they don't spend any money in port or pay for excursions and they eat on board ship. But the US Treasury is clamping down *(see box on page 69)*.

Havana

Cubans are warm and welcoming and, as you can see by the well preserved cars (vintage 1950s), they present a fine example of 'make do and mend'. Exotic and rich in colonial history and vibrating with Latin rhythms, the island is mountainous, rainforested and fringed with white beaches.

 Sailing into the **Terminal Sierra Maestra** at **Havana**, you

Architectural grandeur on Plaza Viejo

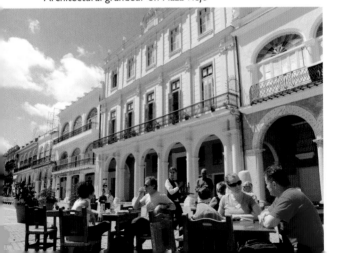

see the 16th-century Spanish defences against the British and French, El Morro and La Cabaña fortresses on the left and La Punta and la Real Fuerza on the right. The terminal has modern facilities

Restrictions

For more information on restrictions for US visitors to Cuba, visit www.treas.gov (the US Treasury website).

and passengers disembark directly onto the cobbled streets of **Habana Vieja** (Old Havana), where tour buses, taxis and horse-drawn carriages await.

Hemingway Haunts

A walk around Habana Vieja will reveal the island's Spanish colonial heritage in all its architectural glory. The best squares to head for are **Plaza de Armas**, the oldest and noted for its second-hand book market as well as its palaces; **Plaza de la Catedral**, with its baroque cathedral, colonial palaces and pavement café, El Patio; and **Plaza Vieja**, newly restored, also with mansions, cafés and a microbrewery. A walk down the main shopping street, **Calle Obispo**, will lead you to **El Floridita**, one of novelist Ernest Hemingway's favourite bars when he lived in Cuba, and then on to the **Parque Central**, where you will find the theatre, fine art museum, hotels and **El Capitolio**.

Grand Cayman

The **Cayman Islands**, 160km (100 miles) or so south of Cuba, consist of three islands that offer some of the most spectacular diving in the world. **Grand Cayman**, the largest at 45km long and 11km wide (28 miles by 7 miles), is where 35,000 people live, as opposed to 1,600 on Cayman Brac and just a handful on Little Cayman. The smaller islands cater mainly for scuba divers.

A British Overseas Department, Grand Cayman is not only a peaceful paradise but is also affluent and sophisticated, with the highest standard of living and the highest per capita income in the Caribbean. Just 750km (480 miles) south of Miami, it is the only one of the three islands that can accept large cruise ships. A few cruise lines start their itineraries here, especially if Cuba *(see page 67)* is one of the ports of call.

George Town

The port's two modern cruise ship terminals are located right in **George Town**, the Cayman Islands' capital. A small but busy commercial town, it has some colonial buildings and is easy to walk around. Taxis are available to take you further afield, or you can opt for an organised excursion.

Grand Cayman is famed for its superlative diving

On the waterfront are the remains of **Fort George**. Built in 1790 to ward off the Spanish, the original fort was made of solid coral rock with walls 1.5 metres (5ft) thick. It was used as a lookout during World War II to keep an eye out for German submarines. Across the street is the **Elmslie United Memorial Church** (Mon–Fri 9am–5pm, Sun 9am–noon). Its timber roof is shaped like an upturned schooner hull with stained-glass windows. Outside the church some of the old stone grave markers resemble little houses.

National Museum

Further along is the popular **Cayman Islands National Museum** (Mon–Fri 9am–5pm, Sat 10am–2pm; charge; tel: 345-949 8368; www.museum.ky) in the 19th-century Old Courts Building, white with green shutters and a bright red roof, which has served as a prison and courthouse. It is the second oldest building in Grand Cayman and a classic example of local architecture. One of the many excellent exhibits is a relief map of the underwaterscape surrounding the islands.

At the Devil's Hang Out in Hell

Opposite, you can see reef life for real, without getting wet, in the **Atlantis *Seaworld Explorer*** (daily, departures on the hour 9am–5pm; charge; tel: 345-949 7700; www.atlantis adventures.com). This is a submarine that takes visitors on an underwater tour 30 metres (100ft) deep.

Further along, the Farmers' and Craft Markets are spilling over with local souvenirs. Look out for jewellery made from caymanite, a semi-precious stone that ranges in colour from beige to pink to brown, that is only found in the Caymans.

Going to Hell

Outside the capital, going north, the road hugs West Bay and Seven Mile Beach, a stretch of white sand attracting wall-to-wall hotels and condos to this bit of paradise, until you get to **Hell**. Yes, the village really is called Hell, due to its surrounding acres of pockmarked limestone rocks that look like the charred remains of an inferno. Consisting only of a petrol

Island dives

The Cayman Islands have plenty of dramatic wall and drop off dives close to the shore, and accessible from a west coast beach. At sea, boats have a choice of 243 permanent moorings.

station, a post office and a few shops and brightly-coloured houses, Hell is a touristy place with plenty of devilish touches, such as a gift shop called the **Devil's Hangout** (daily 7am–5pm), where the owner serves behind the counter dressed as the devil, and at the **Hell Post Office** (Mon–Fri 8.30am–5pm, Sat 8.30am–noon), you can send postcards home from your holiday in Hell.

Turtles and Stingrays

Not far from Hell, the **Turtle Farm** (daily 8.30am–5pm; charge; tel: 345-949 3894; www.turtle.ky) has operated a breed-and-release programme since 1968 and has returned more than 31,000 tagged green turtles to the wild. Take the walkway around the tanks where over 16,000 of the endangered species live and breed.

Off the northern coast and accessible only by tour boats, which leave from a pier near the port, **Stingray City** is considered to be one of the best 3.5-metre (12ft) dive spots in the world. Here stingrays are so used to humans that they will eat squid out of your hands.

Great Gardens

To the east of George Town, on top of a limestone cliff in Savannah, stands **Pedro St James Historic Site** (daily 8.30am–5pm; charge; tel: 345-947 3329; www.pedrostjames.ky), a magnificently restored old stone manor house that's packed with antiques, and has formal English gardens. It was here, in 1835, that the Declaration of Emancipation was read, giving African slaves their freedom.

Inland, **Queen Elizabeth II Botanic Park** (Oct–Mar daily 9am–5.30pm, Apr–Sept until 6.30pm; charge; tel: 345-947 9462; www.botanic-park.ky) is a 26-hectare (65-acre) nature preserve and one of the finest botanical gardens in the Caribbean. More than half of the islands' species of indigenous flora can be found growing naturally in the park.

Jamaica

River trips, powdery beaches, the Blue Mountains, wildlife, gardens and colonial mansions, Jamaica has them all, backed by the irresistible rhythms of reggae and the irrepressible spirit of the people. Cruise ships have a choice of four ports of call at this island – the third largest in the Caribbean – Montego Bay, the main tourism centre, Falmouth, which receives the biggest ships, Ocho Rios, which attracts the majority of ships or smaller Port Antonio in the beautiful east.

Off Doctor's Cave Beach

Enjoying the water at Buccaneer Beach

Montego Bay

Cruise ships dock at the **Freeport** complex 2km (1 mile) or so to the west of **Montego Bay**, or MoBay as it's known, Jamaica's second largest city (after the capital Kingston). The island's hub of tourism, the city sprawls around the bay, with shops, bars and restaurants along the waterfront.

At the modern terminal, the **Freeport Shopping Centre** is a good source for gemstones, watches, cigars, rum and designer labels. Most ships run a shuttle service into town, or you can take an official taxi.

The town square, **Sam Sharpe Square**, is named after Sam 'Daddy' Sharpe, who led slave rebellions in 1831–32 and was hanged by the British. In the square you can still see the stone cell, called the Cage, used to imprison runaway slaves and disorderly sailors.

The Hip Strip

MoBay is dedicated to shopping and partying, and along the seafront on Gloucester Avenue you will find the **Montego Bay Shopping Centre**, the **Craft Market** and a long line of bars and restaurants. Known as the **Hip Strip**, it ends at the busy **Doctor's Cave Beach** (daily; charge) to the north. The beach was made famous in the early 1900s by Dr Alexander

McCatty, who claimed that the water had curative powers, attracting lots of rich Americans. Visitors still flock to the beach, which has good facilities and coral gardens close to the shore that are perfect for snorkelling. At the cyber café there, you can check your email at cheaper rates than on the ship.

Back on the Strip, **Margaritaville**, a noisy, action-packed beach bar, offers Jamaican food and fajitas that you can wash down with any of 52 varieties of margarita. Alternatively, try the sizzling, peppery jerk pork and chicken at the outdoor **Pork Pit**. If you are in port in August you can soak up the atmosphere and island rhythms at **Reggae Sumfest**, a huge five day music festival.

Great Houses

Not far from Montego Bay several plantation houses still stand at the centre of huge estates. The beautifully restored 18th-century **Rose Hall** (daily tours 9am–6pm; charge; www.rosehall.com) was once the home of the alleged 'white witch', Annie Palmer, who is supposed to have murdered three of her husbands.

Nearby, heading eastwards, is **Greenwood Great House** (daily 9am–5pm; charge; www.greenwoodgreathouse.com), which was built by relatives of the poet Elizabeth Barrett Browning in 1800. Greenwood contains a great many antiques and the largest collection of rare musical instruments.

Falmouth

35km (22 miles) east of Montego Bay is the Georgian town of **Falmouth**, home of the newest cruise ship port in Jamaica, which can receive the huge Oasis class ships. The pier is triangular and has

Common sense

Although Jamaica has had some incidents of tourists being robbed at gunpoint, serious incidents are rare. Use common sense and don't go off the beaten track on your own.

Methodist manse

The pretty gingerbread-style Harmony Hall, in St Ann, was a Methodist manse built in the mid-1800s. It is now a gallery showing the work of Caribbean artists, with a shop and a restaurant.

been developed as an 18th-century concept town with cobbled streets, shops, boutiques and restaurants

The old town, from where sugar and rum were shipped, has a fine colonial court house, St Peter's Anglican church and pretty 18th century houses with wrought iron balconies. The Jamaica National Heritage Trust has declared the whole town a National Monument. Tram cars and horse-drawn carriages take visitors on tours around town.

Martha Brae

Excursions from Falmouth include rafting on the beautiful **Martha Brae** river (daily 8.30am–4.30pm; charge; tel: 876-952 0889; www.jamaicarafting.com). Guides will punt you gently downstream on a 30-foot long bamboo raft for two. It takes about an hour to travel the three miles to Martha's Rest at the mouth of the river, about 2 miles (5km) from Falmouth. Overlooking the Martha Brae is the **Good Hope Great House** (daily tours; charge), a fine example of a Georgian plantation house with a commanding view over the surrounding countryside. Tours are available around the house and estate, with its old water wheel, kiln and sugar mill ruins.

Ocho Rios

Known locally as Ochi, **Ocho Rios** is backed by hills of coconut palms and fruit plantations, while its soft, white beaches are protected by colourful coral reefs. The well-equipped cruise ship terminal is within easy walking distance of the town centre, but in the heat, you might prefer to take one of the taxis that line up at port.

In the town centre, a shopping mall, the **Taj Mahal**, has outlets for gemstones, jewellery, designer watches, Blue Mountain coffee and cigars. At the **Olde Craft Market** on Main Street, you can find wood carvings, batik and T-shirts. Everything is overpriced, but friendly haggling is expected.

Fern Gully

Just outside Ochi is **Fern Gully**, a lush, hardwood rainforest where giant ferns and lianas hang over the narrow road. More than 60 species of fern have been recorded here, but they have dwindled a little due to hurricane damage, as well as pollution from traffic.

Ocho Rios is one of the best areas on the island for plant life and has two excellent botanical gardens. **Shaw Park Botanical Gardens** (daily tours 8am–4pm; charge; tel: 876-974 2723; www.shawparkgardens.com) is within walking distance of the port, but on a hill so take a taxi. Its 10 hectares (25 acres) of tropical trees and shrubs surround a lovely waterfall. Nearby, further up the road is the **Coyaba River Garden and Museum** (daily 8am–5pm; charge; tel: 876-974 6235; www.coyaba gardens.com), a lush, tranquil water garden around an interesting Taíno Amerindian museum.

Olde Craft Market artwork

Dunn's River Falls

Dunn's River Falls

Just a 5-minute drive from the terminal, a visit to **Dunn's River Falls** (daily 7am–5pm; charge) will be a cooling experience. In the middle of a rainforest, Dunn's River cascades 180 metres (600ft) down a series of limestone shelves. With an official guide (who will expect a tip), you can join a group to climb up the slippery rocks, stopping for photos by the freshwater pools. You don't have to climb with a guide, but the water is powerful enough in places to make you lose your footing. Wear rubber-soled shoes or hire shoes at the falls.

For a different perspective of the island, you can go on a three-hour excursion on horseback at **Chukka Cove** (tel: 972 2506; www.chukkacaribbean.com), 11km (7 miles) west of Ocho Rios. You will ride along a beautiful beach and through two of the island's oldest sugar estates before stopping at Chukka Cove's private beach for a swim. Polo is played at Chukka Cove and international tournaments take place here during March and April. Alternatively, sign up for the dogsled experience, a two-hour tour in a buggy pulled by enthusiastic dogs to Papillon Cove, the location for scenes with Steve McQueen in the movie, Papillon.

A short drive east of Ocho Rios stands a fine example of a working plantation. **Prospect Estate** (daily, closed 2–3pm; charge) grows bananas, sugar cane, cocoa, coconuts, pineapples and cassava on its 800 hectares (2,000 acres) of land. An estate tour includes the White River Gorge, Sir Harold's Viewpoint, and a grove of memorial trees.

Writers' Retreats

James Bond fans will not want to miss a visit to Oracabessa Bay and **Goldeneye**, the one-time home of the suave hero's creator, novelist and former British Naval Intelligence officer, Ian Fleming (1908–64). The house is now part of a small villa and cottage resort (www.goldeneye.com) and incorporates the predictably named **James Bond Beach Club** (Tue–Sun, 9am–6pm; charge), which has three beaches with good snorkelling, a Jamaican restaurant, water sports and changing rooms. A little further along the coast is **Firefly** (Mon–Thur, Sat 9am–5pm; charge; www.islandoutpost.com/local culture/firefly), the former holiday retreat of another writer, Noël Coward (1899–1973). The house has fantastic views and offers a fascinating insight into the life of the actor, composer and playwright.

The rugged coastline of Port Antonio

Port Antonio

Backed by the Blue Mountains, the twin harbours of the tranquil, secluded town of **Port Antonio** greet the boats as they approach the tropical green rugged coastline of Portland. Cruise ships started docking here when the **Port Antonio Marina** was built in the West Harbour and the **Ken Wright Cruise Ship Pier** was opened in 2002.

In front of the harbour lies the enchanting **Navy Island**, once used by the British Navy but more famously the playground of film star Errol Flynn, who bought it in 1946. Guests attending his wild parties here included Clara Bow, Ginger Rogers and Bette Davis. The island is awaiting redevelopment.

Banana Gold

In the late 18th century, Port Antonio became the banana capital of the world and triggered an exclusive tourist industry when bananas, grown on the foothills of the Blue Mountains, were exported to America by boat from here. The returning banana boats then brought wealthy American visitors back to the island. This was where Harry Belafonte's *Banana Boat Song* originated.

Money does grow on trees

The marina is close to the centre of town, where there is a busy food market (Thur and Sat) in West Street and a shopping mall tucked behind a façade of what looks like a row of Amsterdam canal houses in Fort George Street. From **Christ Church**, built in 1840, in Harbour Street, there is a fine view of the East Harbour. On a peninsular bluff that juts out between the two harbours is **Fort George**, built by the British in 1729 to protect against Spanish invasions.

On the Rio Grande

The **Rio Grande** cuts its way down through dense rainforest to the sea just west of Port Antonio. Bananas from the hillsides were once transported to the port on long bamboo rafts, but the actor Errol Flynn started the craze of riding down the river on them. Today, you can do just the same with a two- to three-hour ride from Berridale to Rafter's Rest (daily 9am–4pm; charge; tel: 914-623 0250).

Dominican Republic

The beautiful southeastern region of the Dominican Republic has a split personality. The coastline is edged with endless white beaches that have become a magnet for large scale, exclusive, all-inclusive tourist development, but venture inland and you find rural simplicity – peasant farmers on horseback tending their cattle and fields of waving sugar cane.

The Spanish-speaking Dominican Republic shares the island, called Hispaniola, with the poverty-stricken and disaster prone French-speaking Haiti. It was the first Caribbean island to be visited by Christopher Columbus in 1492 and **Santo Domingo**, the capital of the Dominican Republic was the first city to be built. Whether your cruise ship docks in Santo Domingo or east of the city at La Romana, a visit to the historic quarter of the capital is worth putting on the agenda. The old town, known as the Zona Colonial, is packed with architectural gems, cobbled streets and historic museums, churches and palaces within what is left of its fortified walls.

La Romana

The port of **La Romana**, established in 1502, is 97km (60 miles) east of the capital. Port facilities are limited and most people opt for a ship excursion, although taxis are available at the terminal for those who want to explore independently. The town is dominated by the country's largest sugar factory, and is just 10km (6 miles) from **Casa de Campo** (House in the Country), one of the most sumptuous holiday resorts in the Caribbean.

This haunt of the rich and famous has three golf courses, a marina, polo club, 15 pools, 17 tennis courts, large riding stables and a beach. Cruise passengers are welcomed on an organised ship excursion, but individuals will find themselves turned away at the big electric iron gates at the entrance.

Above the resort, on the edge of the Chavón Gorge, is the pretty artists' enclave of **Altos de Chavón**, a mock 15th-century Italian village created in the 1980s. The village has a large amphitheatre, seating up to 4,000 people and drawing top performers. The **Museo Arqueológico Regional** (daily 9am–8pm; charge) exhibits a large collection of Amerindian artefacts.

Scuba diving at Serena Cay

Eastern Islas

A 20-minute boat trip from La Romana is **Isla Catalina**, also called **Serena Cay** by some cruise ships. There are no developments on this tropical island, which is dry and flat, but visitors come in their thousands during the cruise ship season. The beach here is protected by a reef, which provides interest for divers and passengers in glass-bottomed boats, and there are plenty of watersports on offer.

A 30-minute drive away, heading south, is the fishing village of **Bayahibe**, its beaches now developed with several all-inclusive hotels as well as hostels for dedicated divers. It sits on the edge of the **Parque Nacional del Este**, where archaeological discoveries have been made dating human habitation of the area to 2000BC. Offshore, but still part of the National Park, is **Isla Saona**. A feature of this trip is the *piscina natural*, a natural swimming pool of waist-deep water formed by a sand bar where boats stop for you to have a swim.

Samaná Peninsula

Cruise ships coming in to the Samaná peninsula on the northeast coast offer a beach excursion to the little island of **Cayo Levantado**. The centre of the island is taken up by an all-inclusive hotel, but at one end there is a broad sweep of sand and palm trees. From January to March, the highlight of any trip to Samaná is **whale watching**. At that time, some 3,000 humpback whales migrate from the north to mate and calve in Samaná Bay, a National Marine mammal sanctuary, and one of the best places in the world for whale watching.

Puerto Rico

At 160km (100 miles) long and 51km (32 miles) wide, Puerto Rico, a US territory, is one of the larger islands in the Caribbean. Its capital **San Juan** is well positioned as a home-port for cruise ships heading south to the islands of the Lesser Antilles in the Eastern Caribbean. With a varied landscape of tropical beaches and densely forested mountains, most of the 4 million inhabitants live in the main towns.

San Juan is the busiest cruise port outside the US mainland. The majority of ships dock at **Calle Marina**, just to the south of **El Viejo San Juan** (Old San Juan), and from here it's an easy walk from the terminal into the most interesting part of the capital city. At the busiest times, some ships have

Price check

San Juan used to be known as a cheap, duty-free port, especially for gold jewellery, but if your cruise is going to St Thomas, it's better to wait as prices are generally better there.

to dock at the Pan American Dock some distance away from the centre, but then a shuttle to Old San Juan is usually provided.

San Juan

To get right to the heart of **Old San Juan**, walk up Calle San Justo. Weatherwise, the town is one of the hottest places in the Caribbean, but you'll find plenty of shade and small, unpretentious cafés serving authentic Puerto Rican cuisine – a variation on traditional Spanish food, with rice and beans the staple dish. The traffic can get so bad that it's not worth taking an air-conditioned coach, you'll see much more on your own. If you get tired you can hop on one of the free trolley buses.

Puerto Rico may have been a US territory for over a century, but not much has changed since the days of Spanish rule in the old town, which dates back to 1521. The narrow, cobbled streets are lined with pretty 16th- and 17th-century Spanish colonial houses with wrought-iron balconies.

Castles and Fortresses

Calle Fortaleza, a busy shopping street full of souvenirs, crosses San Justo; if you turn right you reach **Plaza Colón** (Columbus Square), with a monument commemorating the explorer. Behind the square stands the 17th-century **El Castillo de San Cristóbal** (daily 9am–5pm; guided tours), which has a fascinating history, a network of tunnels and fabulous views of the city. At the other end of the street is the white castellated mansion of **La Fortaleza**, built in 1540 and now the residence of the Governor of Puerto Rico. Soon after the fort was built, the Spanish realised that it didn't give enough protection to the town and set about constructing El Castillo San Felipe del Morro, known as El Morro, on the tip of the peninsula. **El Morro** (daily 9am–6pm; charge) is a hugely atmospheric place – the walls are 6 metres (20ft) thick in places and inside there is a maze of medieval nooks and crannies, as well as a small museum.

Museums and Faith

Back in the old town, it's worth visiting the **Museo de Pablo Casals** (Tue–Sat 9.30am–4.30pm; charge) on Calle San Sebastián, which portrays the life and works of the Catalan cellist, who lived in San Juan from 1957 until his death in 1973. Quite a few good museums are concentrated in this area.

Down Calle del Cristo you come to the classy **Gran Hotel El Convento**, a former Carmelite convent built in the 17th century, but long used as a hotel. Opposite stands the magnificent

The thick walls of El Morro

Juan Ponce de Leon statue
in Old San Juan

San Juan Cathedral (daily 8.30am–4pm), built in 1540 and site of Juan Ponce de León's tomb. He founded the first settlement in 1508 and became the first governor of Puerto Rico. Nearby is **Plaza de Armas**, a replica of Madrid's main square. Trolley buses pass through here and stop right at the cruise pier.

El Yunque

You don't have to go far to find yourself in the rainforest. Designated a National Forest with a network of well-marked trails, **El Yunque** (daily 7.30am–6pm; small charge for El Portal Rain Forest Centre), a 11,000-hectare (27,000-acre) area of rainforest, is home to about 250 species of trees and plants, plus hundreds of frogs and the brilliant Puerto Rican parrot. En route is the palm-fringed **El Luquillo Beach**, the prettiest on the island, where you can snorkel on the reef.

Ponce

If time allows, it is worth visiting **Ponce**, a Spanish colonial town on the south coast, about 90 minutes away. A detour takes you to the massive cave network at **Río Camuy Cave Park** (Wed–Sun 8am–4pm; charge). The best golf courses are about an hour from San Juan; pre-book before your trip.

EASTERN CARIBBEAN

Whichever combination of ports and islands makes up your eastern Caribbean itinerary, there will always be a cosmopolitan flavour to the cruise. From the homeports of San Juan, in Puerto Rico, and Barbados, ships can reach many of the small island ports of the Lesser Antilles in a week.

A visit to a number of islands in this region delivers a heady cultural mix of European, African and indigenous influences. The larger, more developed islands that have become major tourist destinations in their own right, contrast with the smaller islands, which are still off the main tourist track.

It is also in this region that the classic Caribbean islands of our dreams are to be found. The white sandy beaches, fishing boats in hidden coves, and scenic yacht-filled harbours, combine with modern towns and historic neighbourhoods to ensure cruises with a genuinely romantic appeal.

US Virgin Islands

The US Virgin Islands comprises 68 islands, although only four are inhabited: St Thomas, St John, St Croix and Water Island. They are included on both western and eastern Caribbean cruise itineraries and offer the best of both worlds. **St Thomas** is a shopping mecca with the best duty-free goods in the region and **St John**, just a short boat ride away, is mostly one large national park of unspoiled beauty and remains the least developed of the US islands.

Some ships call at St John

Snorkelling in the USVI

Eastern Caribbean

USVI, BVI, Sint Maarten/St-Martin, St-Barths, St Kitts, Antigua, Guadeloupe, Dominica, Martinique, St Lucia, Barbados

Location: The Lesser Antilles are the islands in the Caribbean chain extending from the Virgin islands to Aruba, divided into the Leeward Islands in the north and Windward Islands to the south. The **USVI** (capital Charlotte Amalie) comprise 60+ islands about 64km (40 miles) east of Puerto Rico; The **BVI** (Road Town) comprise 50+ islands. **Sint Maarten/St-Martin** (Philipsburg/Marigot) lies eastwards, north of **St Kitts** (Basseterre); Antigua (St John's) is centrally located between **St-Barths** (Gustavia), St Kitts and **Guadeloupe** (Point-à-Pitre) to the south. Then comes **Dominica** (Roseau), first of the Windward Islands, followed by **Martinique** (Fort-de-France), south of the Tropic of Cancer. **St Lucia** (Castries) lies 35km (21 miles) further south and **Barbados** (Bridgetown) 160km (100 miles) to the southeast, outside the Antillean curve.

Time zone: UTC/GMT -4 (all islands)

Population: 110,000 (USVI); 24,500 (BVI); 81,650 (Sint Maarten/St Martin); 8,823 (St-Barths); 50,300 (St Kitts); 87,884 (Antigua); 405,500 (Guadeloupe); 73,600 (Dominica); 398,000 (Martinique); 173,765 (St Lucia); 255,800 (Barbados).

Language: English (USVI, Antigua, Barbados); English/Creole (BVI, St Kitts, Dominica, St Lucia); French/Creole (Guadeloupe, Martinique, St-Martin), Dutch (Sint Maarten); English is also spoken in Sint Maarten/St-Martin.

Money matters: USVI, BVI: US$; Sint Maarten/St-Martin, St-Barths, Martinique, Guadeloupe: euro; St Kitts, Antigua, Dominica, St Lucia: EC$; Barbados: BDS$. US dollars are accepted in all islands.

Telephone & Internet: Country codes: +340 (usvi); +284 (bvi); +599 (Sint Maarten); +596 (St-Martin); +590 (St-Barths); +869 (St Kitts); +268 (Antigua); +767 (Dominica); +596 (Martinique); +590 (Guadeloupe); +758 (St Lucia); +246 (Barbados). Internet is widely available in the main towns and hotels.

Yachts docked at St Thomas

instead of St Thomas, but experienced cruise visitors to the latter know that they should do their shopping in the morning in Charlotte Amalie, the capital, and then take a short ferry ride to St John for an afternoon on one of its glorious beaches. **St Croix**, out on a limb to the south, is a complete contrast to St Thomas, quieter and less developed with a marine national park and a varied landscape, from grassy hills to lush rainforest.

St Thomas

Although a few ships anchor in the bay when stopping off at **St Thomas**, and tender passengers into the heart of the capital, **Charlotte Amalie**, most berth at **Havensight Dock**, just over 2km (1 mile) east of town. Barely off the ship, you can start intensive retail therapy in **Havensight Mall** at the dock, for every major duty-free retailer has an outlet here as well as in the capital's shopping centre.

Crown Bay, on the other side of the harbour, about twice as far from the capital as Havensight, is also used on busy days. The port area has a replica sugar mill and other facilities but the shops at Crown Bay Center are not as extensive as at Havensight. The ferry to **Water Island**, the fourth US Virgin Island, leaves from Crown Bay Marina.

Charlotte Amalie

Scores of taxis wait by the dockside – not all official, but all operating on a shared basis. Progress will be slow driving into **Charlotte Amalie**, so if you can, you might as well walk. Just follow the road along the seafront.

The capital has one of the most attractive harbours in the region, especially when the sun sets behind the sails of the yachts filling the bay. Behind the wharf, where ferries depart for St John, stands **Fort Christian** and the **Virgin Islands**

Sunrise on Morning Star beach, St Thomas

Museum (Mon–Fri 8.30am– 4.30pm; donations). Built by the Danes in 1680, it is the oldest building in continuous use on the island. Behind the museum, **Emancipation Gardens** marks the start of shop-filled **Dronningens Gade** (Main Street), which has endless alleyways running down to the waterfront,

Take the tram

For a good view of Charlotte Amalie, take the Paradise Point Tramway – a seven-minute cable car ride to a viewing platform 210 metres (700ft) up. The tramway station is just across the road from Havensight Mall.

each with a mini-shopping mall. At No. 14 stands the house where Impressionist artist Camille Pissarro was born in 1830, which is now a small **art gallery** selling paintings and prints by local and regional artists.

Castle on the Hill

Although richer in shops than historical sights, Charlotte Amalie does have a legacy of piracy, and what is left of **Blackbeard's Castle** is at the top of several long flights of steps cut into the hillside. Built by the Danes in 1679, it was supposed to have been used by the notorious English pirate, Edward Teach, aka Blackbeard.

Close by, off Kongens Gade (Government Hill), is the **Seven Arches Museum** (Mon–Sat 10am–4pm or by appointment; donations welcome; tel: 304-774 9295; www.sevenarchesmuseum.co), a restored 19th-century Danish artisan's house portraying Denmark's colonisation of the islands, with authentic furnishings and interior, and a balcony view of the harbour. It is named after the seven arches that support the staircase.

The Danes were the first Europeans to settle in St Thomas and St John in the 17th century and eventually sold the islands to the US in 1917 for US$25 million.

Across the Island

The majority of excursions are on the water, involving sailing or kayaking, swimming, snorkelling and scuba diving in beautifully clear waters awash with colourful marine life. It's cheaper to hire a taxi independently rather than through the ship, or hire a car if you want to go further afield. The rates are fixed so you don't need to haggle.

To the north of the capital is the **St Peter Greathouse and Botanical Gardens** (daily 8am–4pm, last entry 3.30pm; charge; tel: 340-774-4999; www.greathousevi.com) where you can walk through the 4 hectares (11 acres) of landscaped gardens. At about 305 metres (1,000ft) above sea level, you can see up to 24 islands.

Lorikeet arboreal parrot

At **Coral World Ocean Park** (Nov–Mar daily 9am–4pm, times vary the rest of the year; charge), 15 minutes from Havensight on the northeast coast, a three-level underwater observatory gives a fish's eye view of an enormous range of marine life, and it's fun to watch the divers at feeding time.

St John

A visit to the neighbouring island of **St John** is one of the most popular excursions, either as part of a tour or on your own. Two-thirds of St John is an unspoilt national park (gifted to the US by the Rockefellers) with 110 different types of tree and many species of birds and butterflies. It also has more than 40 beaches and coves with an eco-resort at **Caneel Bay**. The best, though, is **Trunk Bay**, which has an underwater snorkelling trail, giving you a chance to snorkel round the coral reef.

Regular ferries cross from Charlotte Amalie (45 minutes) and from Red Hook (about 25 minutes from Havensight) on the east coast. These are cheaper and more frequent.

St Croix

Large cruise ships arrive at **St Croix** (pronounced Croy, as in boy) on the west coast at the modern 450-metre (1,500ft) pier in **Frederiksted**, where you'll find a handful of shops, the renovated 18th century **Fort Frederik**, with its museum and art gallery, and the **Caribbean Museum Center for the Arts** (Wed–Sat 10am–4pm; tel: 340-772 2622; www.cmcarts. org) promoting regional art. The capital, **Christiansted**, a shuttle bus ride away, on the north coast, has more shops, bars and restaurants in **King's Alley Walk**, but only the smaller ships can call here.

At 212 sq km (82 sq miles), St Croix is larger than St Thomas, but it is less developed, and far less crowded. It is well known for its magnificent beaches – **Sandy Point**, **Cane Bay** and **Davis Bay** – a short coach or taxi ride from Frederiksted. **Salt River Bay National Historic Park**, on the north coast, is the site of a Columbus landing – the only one on US territory. It has a huge mangrove forest and an underwater canyon which is ideal for scuba diving.

Some of the best places to visit include the **Cruzan Rum Distillery**, the **St George Village Botanical Garden** (Nov–May daily 9am–5pm, June–Oct Tue–Sat 9am–5pm; charge), set among the ruins of a plantation village, and the restored **Whim Great House** (Mon–Sat; charge), which portrays plantation life during Danish rule.

British Virgin Islands

However you choose to spend your time ashore in the British Virgin Islands, it won't be hurried. These volcanic outcrops are Robinson Crusoe-style havens rich in banana trees, palms and mangoes, garlanded with white sandy beaches and secret coves set in a perfect sea, and all you can do here is revel in it.

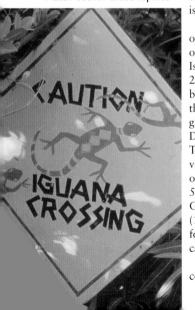

Watch out for those reptiles

There is very little development to spoil it all. Most of the 50 or so British Virgin Islands are uninhabited, the 24,500-strong population being concentrated on the three biggest – Tortola, Virgin Gorda and Jost Van Dyke. The topography of Tortola and Virgin Gorda is very rugged and mountainous: Tortola's Mount Sage is 536 metres (1,709ft) and Gorda Peak 414 metres (1,369ft), not good terrain for building high-rise hotels, casinos and shopping malls.

These islands have become a haven for 'yachties',

who sail among them and know what it's like to have a beach that's inaccessible by land to themselves.

Tortola

Most cruise lines visit **Tortola** but only the small-ship cruise companies tend to stop at Virgin Gorda and Jost Van Dyke. Ships usual-

> ### US currency
> When other British islands gained independence in the 1960s and 1970s, the BVI remained a self-governing British Overseas Territory, along with Montserrat and Anguilla. To maintain economic ties with the USVI, the US dollar is used as currency.

ly tender passengers ashore in the harbour of the pretty capital of Road Town. A road around the 54-sq km (21-sq mile) island was completed in the early 1980s and, with a line of taxis offering round-trip tours, it's relatively easy to explore.

Road Town

What we would probably consider a village, **Road Town** is not most people's idea of a capital city. Along **Main Street** – five minutes' walk from the pier and yachting marina at Wickhams Cay – many of the traditional, Caribbean wooden houses have been restored and house several shops. There is a lively crafts market, where you'll find brightly coloured mobiles, driftwood napkin rings and other fun items. On the waterfront, the landmark **Pusser's Pub**, an attractive gingerbread-style building, offers English food and the Pusser's Painkiller, a notorious rum cocktail.

Island Tours and Beaches

If you're not after isolation, for a whole beach experience go to **Cane Garden Bay**, where **Rhymers'** restaurant serves tasty seafood, makes great barbecues and provides showers, towels and some water sports facilities (for a charge), including windsurfing, especially in November's perfect conditions. Some

Snorkelling at The Baths, Tortola

ships offer excursions on open-air safari buses, which include a stop at the beach. Local companies organise boat and snorkelling tours and sailing trips from the pier in Road Town.

For a walk with wonderful vistas, visit the **Mount Sage National Park**, where you can hike along a rainforest trail. On the way back, stop at **Skyworld** for a 360-degree view of Tortola and the surrounding islands.

Virgin Gorda

The tiny but beautiful island of **Virgin Gorda** lies 20km (12 miles) from Tortola and plenty of boats go there from Road Town's pier, docking at **Spanish Town**. On the other side of the small shopping plaza is the **Virgin Gorda Yacht Harbour**, where you can eat and admire the view at the **Bath and Turtle Pub**.

The most popular attraction here is **The Baths**, in the **Devil's Bay National Park**, a magical beach where gigantic boulders have formed grottoes and salt-water pools. An easy trail runs through it all. Ships often offer excursions to The Baths, or you could negotiate with one of the taxi drivers at Spanish Town for a round-trip fare there. Alternatively, you can take a taxi to the island's best beach, **Spring Bay**, a good place for some excellent snorkelling.

Arriving at **Jost Van Dyke** is like stepping into a time warp: a clutch of houses in a bay surrounded by green hills, and goats grazing in the cemetery. A water taxi will take you round to the blissful beach at White Bay.

Sint Maarten

The Netherlands are in bed with France on the tiny island of **Sint Maarten/St-Martin** and have been peacefully so for more than 200 years. The border divides the smallest land mass – 96 sq km (37 sq miles) – in the world shared by two countries, and they couldn't be more different. The smaller Dutch Sint Maarten is brash with large resorts, casinos and fast food joints, whereas the French St-Martin is prettier, quieter and more sophisticated, with Parisian-style shops and cafés.

Philipsburg

Most of the major cruise lines include **Philipsburg**, the capital of Sint Maarten, as a port of call. Some people may recognise it from the film *Speed 2: Cruise Control*, in which a ship (*Seabourn Legend* in real life) crashes dramatically into the harbour front. The **Pointe Blanche cruise terminal** is just 2km

Strolling down Old Street

Eat at l'Escargot, St Maarten

(1 mile) away from the town centre and is well furnished with shops, facilities and taxis – opt for a multi-passenger minibus for a cheaper ride into the centre. Sometimes ships anchor in the bay and tender passengers right to the pier in town.

It's easy to find your way around Philipsburg. The town curves around Great Bay Beach and a board walk makes this a pleasant stroll. There are only two streets, running parallel to the waterfront and one is called **Voorstraat** (Front Street), the other **Achterstraat** (Back Street). These are the main shopping areas and tend to get very crowded when cruise ship passengers descend on the duty-free port, which has designer boutiques and traditional architecture. **Old Street** is one of many lanes *(steegjes)* connecting the two, and here you will find pretty, alfresco restaurants and the **Old Street Shopping Centre**, a small mall with more than 20 shops as well as restaurants.

Shopping Treats

In **Wathey Square** (De Ruyterplein), which faces the pier, there's a late 18th-century courthouse, and some beautiful old buildings decorated with traditional West Indian gingerbread fretwork. A lively market, a selection of restaurants and plenty more shops make this a place to head for, along with the little lanes, lined with more boutiques, cafés and the occasional courtyard, spilling over with tropical plants.

Among the best buys is jewellery, which is reasonably priced (as it is throughout the Caribbean). Posh shops sell Gucci and other designer goods as well as alcohol and leather products at duty-free prices – although not as low as they are in St Thomas. But for a real taste of the West Indies, look in at a local store crammed with spices, cane sugar, batik clothing, handwoven hammocks, local crafts and guavaberry liqueur, the local rum-based firewater made from wild red berries, which can spike up a cocktail.

ST-MARTIN

The smaller cruise ships sometimes anchor outside Marigot, the capital of the prettier French side of the island, and tender passengers in to the harbour. Otherwise, unless your time in Sint Maarten is very short, try to get over here and experience

Best Beaches

The most convenient beaches are Great Bay – just along from Philipsburg's Front Street – and Little Bay, slightly further west, but they may both be crowded. For more privacy, take a taxi further afield to Simpson Bay Beach (good for water sports and for gambling, as the nearby Pelican Resort has a big casino); Dawn Beach (great for snorkelling); or Maho Bay Beach, where you can sunbathe in style or play the tables at the Maho Bay Hotel and Casino.

On the French side, Baie Orientale is gorgeous, with good beachside cafés and a classic French Riviera atmosphere. Baie Rouge is best for snorkellers, while Baie Longue is uncrowded. Clothing is optional on most beaches on the French side.

the difference between the two parts. Big cruise ships usually offer a tour to Marigot from Philipsburg with a detour through the district of Orléans to visit **La Ferme des Papillons** (daily 9am–3.30pm; charge; www.thebutterflyfarm.com) a butterfly farm featuring a fascinating collection of species from around the world. Another option from Philipsburg is a drive to the lovely French **Baie Orientale** for a swim, sunbathing (chairs provided) and a leisurely lunch.

Marigot

 Much less commercialised than Philipsburg, **Marigot** really feels like a French seaside resort. It has colourful markets and a broad, beautiful harbour overlooked by restaurants and cafés featuring the best of Caribbean and French cuisine. Several offer a good lunchtime Créole set menu. Then walk off the meal with a 15-minute stroll up to the ruins and views from **Fort St Louis**.

The stylish shops can be found in rue de la République, rue de la Liberté and the **Marina Port La Royale**, where there are more smart cafés looking out at the yachts.

If you have a full day ashore, you could take a taxi tour of the island or a cab from Philipsburg to Marigot. Negotiate the fare in advance (US dollars are accepted) and ask the driver to build in waiting time, or come back at a specified hour if you want to stop at a beach or a restaurant.

Spoilt for choice

Foodies should schedule a trip to Grand Case in the north of St-Martin. This little town offers more than its fair share of places to eat, and is reputed to have more restaurants than inhabitants.

St-Barthélemy

The essence of France in a paradise on earth is how St-Barthélemy has often been described and its reputation as a quintessential hideaway for the rich and famous has meant that its 26 sq km (10 sq miles) of land provides some of the most sought after property in the world.

Vibrant frangipani

With 22 beaches and coves to choose from, many of them empty, windy cliff-side walks, nature reserves and salt marshes, it's easy to get away from it all in St-Barths, as it is affectionately called. Chic, stylish and sophisticated in the way that only the French know how, it remains unpretentious with simple architecture – no big hotels here – reflecting the island's casual atmosphere.

Gustavia

Only the smaller cruise ships can call at St-Barths, dropping anchor in the outer harbour at **Gustavia**, the island's capital. Tenders take passengers to **L'Espace Gambier**, a small welcome centre at the entrance to the port where you can find a taxi, book an excursion or pick up a walking tour.

Picturesque, red-roofed buildings climb up the steep hill behind, harbouring duty-free shops with the latest Paris fashions all available in the exclusive boutiques, and funky bars and pavement cafés full of people chilling and spilling out on to the streets.

From the late 18th to 19th century, the island was occupied by the Swedes, hence the name Gustavia. In 1784 Louis XVI gave the island to Sweden in exchange for trading rights in the port of Gothenburg. This was a stroke of good luck for the islanders as it meant they were spared the terrors of the French Revolution a few years later, which spread to the

The harbour in Gustavia

other islands of the French West Indies. The Swedes left the island the forts: Oscar, Karl and Gustav, and beneath Fort Oscar is the **Historical Museum of St-Barthélemy** (Mon–Fri and Sat am; closed for lunch; charge), which provides a history of the island.

Eating at the Beach

There are few things better than having a long relaxed lunch on a beautiful beach, and this is possible at **Shell Beach**, which, as its name suggests, is a shell-covered stretch of gleaming sand within walking distance of Gustavia, near the ruins of Fort Karl.

The most popular beach at **St Jean**, on the north coast, is backed by shops, hotels and bistros, but is rarely crowded. The luxury **Eden Rock Hotel** stands on a spit of rock dividing the beach at St Jean in two.

Another good beach, and one of the most secluded, is

Colombier at the tip of the northwest peninsula, where turtles nest every year. It can only be reached by boat from Gustavia or a half-hour walk from Colombier village.

St Kitts

Travellers in search of the 'real' West Indies won't be disappointed with St Kitts, which crams an astonishing range of terrain – from cane fields to rainforest and mountains – into its 170 sq km (65 sq miles). With a laid-back atmosphere and a varied history, the slow rhythm of this miniature nation has to be infectious.

Arriving at the **Port Zante Cruise Terminal**, with its duty-free shops, restaurants and casino in the heart of the graceful capital, **Basseterre**, you can walk right off the ship and into the town.

Dependent on tourism, the astute islanders have restored many of Basseterre's gingerbread-trimmed public buildings and homes to their former glory, giving the palm-filled town an olde worlde charm. **Independence Square**, a former slave market and now an attractive park surrounded by 18th-century houses, is particularly worth a look; as is the **Circus** traffic intersection on Fort Street, with a clock-tower of elaborately-worked cast iron in the centre. You can watch it all from the balcony of one of Basseterre's liveliest restaurants, **Ballahoo**, well-known for its spare ribs.

Wander through the back streets off Bay Road and you'll find goats and chickens wandering free and roadside stalls selling fish, fruit and flowers. The town has a few galleries stocked with good-quality art, crafts and antiques.

The best local buys are leather and cotton goods, spices, pottery and sea opal jewellery; Fort Street and Liverpool Row are good places for unusual finds. Those who prefer brand name shopping may find something in the Pelican Shopping Mall.

Sugar cane fields surround a church on St Kitts

St Kitts Scenic Railway

A 49km (30-mile) narrow gauge railway encircles St Kitts, which mostly basks in a sleepy haze, with fields of sugar cane rising up to the edge of the rainforest around Mount Liamuiga (1,156 metres/3,792ft). Built between 1912 and 1926 to transport sugar cane to the sugar mill in Basseterre, the sugar mill has closed but the railway line is back in action with a comfortable double decker train equipped to take visitors on a circular tour around the island in just four hours with a better view than you get from the road. The **St Kitts Scenic Railway** links up to the cruise lines' timetables and is a wonderful way to see the island. For those wanting to see more, taxi drivers offer tours of the island too, and can include a stop for lunch. Check the rates listed in the cruise terminal, as they are not displayed in cabs, and establish the fare with the driver first.

Driving westward from Basseterre, you come to **Romney Manor** (Old Road Town; tel: 869-465 6253; www.caribelle

batikstkitts.com), 2.4 hectares (6 acres) of glorious gardens containing a saman tree believed to be more than 350 years old, so big it covers half an acre. In the grounds of the plantation is the **Caribelle Batik** factory where you can see hand-printed fabrics being made, using a traditional Indonesian process. A three-minute walk from Romney Manor is **Wingfield Estate**, with the ruins of a sugar mill and rum distillery. Wingfield is the place to come for **Sky Rides** zip line tour (tel: 869-466 4259; www.skysafarist kitts.com), where cables allow you to fly over Wingfield River through the rainforest.

Further along the road is **Brimstone Hill National Park** (daily 9.30am–5.30pm; charge; www.brimstonehillfortress. org), a huge fortress, with a small museum, from where you can see the two volcanic cones of St Eustatius and Saba to the northwest. The British called this 'the Gibraltar of the West Indies' until it was captured for nearly a year by the French in 1782. For lunch, you can stop at **Rawlins Plantation Inn**, with its wonderful gardens, on the island's northern slopes; or **Ottley's Plantation Inn**, on the Atlantic side, which has a spring-fed pool and rainforest trails.

Contrasting Beaches

For a day on the beach, head for the southeastern peninsula. **Frigate Bay**, a long stretch of soft white sand is a complete contrast to the black sand beaches further north. There is an 18-hole championship golf course here and lots of hotels. Beyond it is **Friar's Bay**, a narrow strip of land divided by the road where you can enjoy a unique experience of swim-

Music event

The St Kitts Music Festival is a well-organised spectacular four-night event held every June, and features top Caribbean artists from every musical genre.

ming in the Atlantic Ocean on one side and the Caribbean Sea on the other. Towards the end of the peninsula is **Turtle Beach**, a paradise for bird-watchers and nature lovers and where visitors can snorkel, go kayaking or windsurf. Power boats are available to take you further around the coast or to the neighbouring island of Nevis.

Nevis

Ferries regularly leave Basseterre for the 45-minute, 20km (12-mile) journey to the tiny island of **Nevis**, where Horatio Nelson married Fanny Nisbet in 1787. The trip is an experience in itself – you can travel in style or share the cargo boat with livestock and sacks of vegetables.

Fishing boats, Nevis

The ferry docks in **Charlestown**, which has beautifully restored, pastel-tinted, gingerbread-trimmed houses with tropical gardens. Here, street vendors will tempt you with fruit wines made from gooseberry, sorrel and pawpaw (papaya) – but beware the island's speciality hot pepper sauce if you don't have an asbestos tongue. You can also buy colourful batik, pottery and unusual handicrafts at the **Cotton Ginnery** on the waterfront. For a lovely beach and a good lunch, take a taxi to **Pinney's Beach**, a short hop from Charlestown.

Some cruise lines offer excursions to Nevis, which may include a rainforest hike to **Nevis Peak**. If you prefer to go independently, *do* check the return ferry schedules to allow plenty of time to get back to the ship.

Fishing in the shadow of Nevis Peak

Antigua

Since the demise of the sugar industry, the 270-sq-km (108-sq-mile) heart-shaped island of Antigua has come to depend on tourism. With the ever increasing sizes of cruise liners, the island has built three quays in **St John's: Redcliffe** and **Heritage** quays and **Nevis Street Pier**. Ever conscious of the desire to give visitors a variety of things to do, Antigua offers much beyond beach, boat or shopping trips.

St John's

Ships dock in the centre of the island's pretty capital, set around a large natural harbour. Historic Redcliffe's picturesque quay offers a range of shops and restaurants in a pleasantly shaded setting of restored wooden buildings, with lattice-work balconies. By the other two quays is a breezy, pastel-coloured mall, with an air-conditioned casino and duty-free shops. Between them, local traders selling sarongs, T-shirts and sunhats are gathered under the roof of the **Vendors' Mall**.

Three centuries ago, the scene was very different. The 'passengers' tripping off the gangplanks were enslaved men and women from West Africa, who were lined up for sale to plantation owners.

Alongside the shops and restaurants, the port-side area provides banking and telecommunication facilities, which are located on High and Long streets. Island cash tills readily swallow US dollars, although paying with local currency (Eastern Caribbean dollars) normally means slightly lower prices, once the exchange rates have been calculated.

A Wander Round Town

With its single-storey wooden houses in muted hues, flanking the narrow lanes, St John's offers the perfect chance to explore the urban Caribbean.

Take an early morning start, and grab a coffee and cake from one of the excellent local bakeries or cafés in lower St Mary's Street or Redcliffe Quay. You will catch the cool of the day and obtain an insight into the intriguing events of a small Caribbean island.

Heritage Quay, St John's.

Island Heritage

A few minutes from the quayside, the former courthouse on Long Street, solidly built in 1747 from local stone, is now the **Museum of Antigua and Barbuda** (Mon–Fri 8.30am–4pm, Sat 10am–2pm; donations; tel: 268-462 1469; www.antigua museums.org). The renovated building is packed with local heritage. Exhibits in the airy main hall highlight island life and history, while next door houses a database of monument inscriptions from around Antigua and the associated isle of Barbuda.

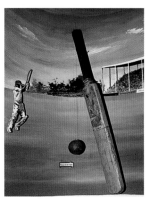

Viv Richards' cricket bat on display in the museum

The Anglican **Cathedral of St John the Divine**, a few minutes further up Long Street, originally dates from 1683 but, like so many buildings, it was damaged and restored after a severe earthquake in 1834. The landmark towers of this striking baroque edifice have long proclaimed St John's presence to new arrivals.

Across the road, the **Antigua Recreation Ground** is the hallowed home of Antiguan cricket, and the spot where local sporting hero Sir Vivian Richards – the 'Master Blaster' – knocked off the fastest century in cricket. His bat is on display at the Museum of Antigua and Barbuda. However, a new ground with higher specifications, named after Sir Viv Richards, was built for the 2007 World Cup further out to the airport and Test Matches are now held there.

Return down Redcliffe and St Mary's streets, the **Ebenezer Methodist Church** was completed in 1839, but twice restored after earthquakes rattled its foundations. On Market Street, opposite the West Bus Station, you can buy tropical fruits in the covered **Heritage Market** and craftwork in the building next door.

Out of Town

Nowhere is far away in Antigua, but the full range of stunning beaches and historic sites lies out of walking distance. Cycling will get you a bit further under your own steam, and the best biking destination is **Fort Bay**, a leisurely 20-minute ride northeast of the town centre. Continue along Popeshead Street and turn left at the sign for Miller's-by-the-Sea to reach this popular locals' beach. At the southern end of the promontory, **Fort James** dates from 1739 and guards perfect views out to sea.

Sugar mills at Betty's Hope

English Harbour

Further afield, at English Harbour to the southeast, lies one of Antigua's most historic attractions, **Nelson's Dockyard** (daily 8am–5pm; charge). It's about 30 minutes away from St John's by local bus from the West Bus Station or by taxi (check the fixed rates). A series of beautifully restored mid-18th century buildings give this harbour an historic atmosphere. It was once a key command post for the

British Navy, and where Admiral Horatio Nelson was based while he commanded HMS *Boreas*.

The stunning bay is overlooked by the impressive fortifications of **Fort Shirley** (daily; combined ticket with the Dockyard), where there

Sail away

English Harbour is the focal point of Antigua Sailing Week held each April, when yachting enthusiasts from all over the world converge on the island for some top-class sailing – and partying.

is a lookout spot known as **Shirley Heights**. It comes alive with the music of reggae and steel pan bands, and barbecues on Sunday evening.

Sugar Museum

Taxi drivers offer a tour of the whole island, but if time is limited, it's worth slowing down to savour one or two sites. **Betty's Hope** (Pares Village; Tue–Sat 10am–4pm; charge), on the loop back from English Harbour, was built in the 1650s as the first sugar plantation on the island. Remnants of sugar mills are scattered across the island, but here the sugar mill has been restored and occasionally grinds the cane in full sail. Other plantation buildings remain in ruins for lack of finance, but there is a small visitor's centre.

To the east, the natural limestone arch of **Devil's Bridge** and art gallery of **Harmony Hall**, a former plantation house, offer interesting stops en route to the sands of **Half Moon Bay**.

Every Antiguan promotes a favourite beach, and with a beach for every day of the year around the island, competition is tough. Darkwood Beach, Hawksbill Bay and Ffryes Bay on the west coast are all strong contenders.

If you have the time and feel energetic enough, **Boggy Peak** (402 metres/1,319ft), Antigua's highest point, is a rewarding 2-hour hike in the southwest of the island. Ask to be dropped off at the start of the track just beyond Urlings.

Clothes shops in Le Moule on Grande Terre

Guadeloupe

A piece of the Republic of France, Guadeloupe is a butterfly-shaped island that is a French *département* and, although you will breathe in the unmistakable tropical air as you leave the ship, you will undeniably be entering a part of the European Union, where the euro is currency and the lingo is French.

Divided in two by the slender Rivière Salée, the eastern region, Grande-Terre, is a lush land rich in banana plantations, cane fields and gentle hills, but with a stormy, wind-battered Atlantic coastline. It is also reasonably well developed with hotels and beach resorts. Basse-Terre to the west is a dramatically mountainous region, with a live volcano, La Soufrière, and dense forests holding more attractions for hikers and nature lovers. The seas are calm and the beaches are white and glorious. You cross from one region to the other via a drawbridge across the strait.

None of these wonderful attributes will be apparent, however, when you first emerge from the cruise terminal in the capital, **Pointe-à-Pitre**. Although you'll find some nice facilities at the port – including landscaped gardens and duty-free stores, with more shops and small markets close by, it is not a friendly place and you will need to negotiate heavy traffic to explore the main town. Opinions vary as to whether it's worth the effort. If you like your towns neat and pretty, you won't want to waste much time here. But if you enjoy seedy grandeur and a down-to-earth, hard-working atmosphere, you could let the town work its charm.

Pointe-à-Pitre

In the **Place de la Victoire**, a short stroll along the waterfront, are some elaborate French colonial houses, complete with balconies and shutters, and the pretty harbour of **La Darse**, which lies off the square. Here is the main tourist information office, which is worth popping into since Guadeloupe is not the easiest island to explore on your own. There is also a small but helpful information bureau in the cruise terminal, where you can pick up local maps, find a scrupulous taxi guide, perhaps, and get useful advice on getting about.

If your ship docks early, go to the rue St-John Perse to find the town's covered market, **Le Marché Couvert**. It is at its colourful best in the morning. Here you can find stylish cotton clothing and fabric, straw bags and local crafts and feast your senses at stalls piled high with fragrant

Taxi fares

You'll have to negotiate hard over taxi fares in Pointe-à-Pitre if you want to explore on your own. Fares are regulated and should be listed at taxi stands, but it's always best to agree a firm price before you begin your tour, or ask the tourist bureau at the port to find you a co-operative driver.

spices and exotic fruits and vegetables, then head off for a coffee, a pastry and a chance to watch the world go by from a café. Just as you would in France, you must expect to pay for everything in euros, not US dollars, so either take a good supply with you or get some from an ATM onshore.

For more serious shopping, the rues Schoelcher, Nozières and Frébault have the best boutiques, while the **Distillerie Bellevue** on rue Bellevue Damoiseau is the best place to sample and buy Rhum Agricole, the island's distinctive falling-down water, which locals claim will not give you a hangover because it's made from pure cane sugar juice – but don't take that too seriously.

As it's part of France, Guadeloupe offers the best bargains for perfume, crystal-ware, cosmetics and fashion accessories from French design houses; prepare to stock up on Lalique, Hermès, Dior, Chanel, and French lingerie.

Créole Specialities

With its French Créole heritage, Guadeloupe is a great place to eat; you can sample crayfish, stuffed crab and even sea oyster omelettes, and the local specialities of goat curry and black pudding, or *boudin*. The best places to enjoy lunch with a view, are at Grande Anse, in northwest Basse-Terre, and La Marina at **Bas-du-Fort**, just outside Pointe-à-Pitre.

Two museums worth visiting are the **Musée de St-John Perse** (rue Achille Rene-Boisneuf; Mon–Fri 9am–5pm, Sat 8.30pm–12.30pm; charge), a beautiful, and lovingly re-stored colonial building commemorating the work of the island's Nobel Prize-winning poet; while the **Musée Schoelcher** (rue Peynier; Mon–Fri 9am–5.30pm; charge) celebrates the life and anti-slavery campaigns of Victor Schoelcher, a leading 19th-century abolitionist. Afterwards, head northeast to the Place de l'Eglise to see the exquisite stained-glass (and apparently hurricane-proof) windows of the **Cathédrale de St-Pierre et St-Paul**, which has a flower market near its entrance.

Grande-Terre

The advantage of arriving at Pointe-à-Pitre is that it lies in the middle of the island near to the bridge over the Rivière Salée in the south, and is well-placed for exploring both Grande-Terre and Basse-Terre. A 10-minute taxi ride will take you to **La Marina** at **Bas-du-Fort**, where you'll find an attractive marina surrounded by shops, restaurants and cafés. Here, you can hire a motorboat or join an excursion to tour Guadeloupe's mangrove swamps, or visit a giant aquarium (daily 9am–7pm; charge) which houses more than 900 types of Caribbean sea creatures.

Wearing colourful Antillean Creole dress

Further east from Pointe-à-Pitre, on Grande-Terre's south coast, lies **Le Gosier**, which has 8km (5 miles) of beach bordered by some of the region's best resorts. A spectacular 18th-century fortress, **Fort Fleur-d'Epée**, commands fine views from here. Continue on to **Pointe des Chateaux** at the easternmost tip of the island, and you'll discover breathtaking, craggy coastal scenery beaten into castle-like formations by the fierce Atlantic waves.

Suspended walkways in the Parc Naturel

Basse-Terre

The best beach in Basse-Terre – and, indeed, on the whole island – is **Grande Anse** on the northwest coast, though **Deshaies** (slightly to the south) is good for snorkelling.

Further inland nature lovers will be captivated by Basse-Terre's huge **Parc Naturel de la Guadeloupe**, where you can enjoy a hike and a swim beneath a crystal clear waterfall, **Cascade de l'Ecrevisse**. Just driving along the winding coast road bordering the park is a delight in itself. Many cruise ships organise short jungle hikes through rainforest as part of an excursion.

The focal point of the park is **La Soufrière** volcano, soaring 1,467 metres (4,812ft) above sea level. To reach its peak (if you dare) you'll have to drive up twisting roads past banana trees and exotic vegetation, stopping en route to view the lovely tropical gardens at **St-Claude**. The road ends at 1,000 metres (3,300ft), but hikers can walk the rest of the way and have the rather scary experience of feeling the ground beneath their feet grow hotter, and the rotten-egg smell of sulphur grow more intense, as they climb.

East of Soufrière are **Les Chutes du Carbet**, with three cascades at 115 metres (380ft), 110 metres (360ft) and 20 metres (65ft) it is believed to be the highest waterfall in the Caribbean. To reach the falls requires a forest hike, so you'd be advised to join a guided tour.

Before heading back to the port along the east coast you can stop at **Trois Rivières** to see the **Parc Archéologique des Roches Gravées** – ancient rocks etched with images of men and animals, which were carved by the Amerindians who originally inhabited Guadeloupe.

Trips to the Islands

From Trois Rivières, two ferries a day make the 25-minute trip to Les Saintes, where in 1872 Britain's Admiral Rodney defeated the French in the Battle of the Saints. Only two of the eight islands are inhabited, and they are sparsely populated by the descendants of Breton pirates who took refuge there. Boats from Point-à-Pitre also go to Les Saintes as well as the circular Marie-Galante, named after Columbus's ship and bordered by white sandy beaches.

Réserve Cousteau

Most cruise lines offer three- to four-hour tours around one or both parts of the island, and to Soufrière, often including lunch. But one of the most eye-opening trips is to the **Réserve Cousteau** off Malendure on the west coast, a marine park set up by the French underwater explorer Jacques Cousteau in 1955. Here, a spectacular underwater world has been created by the hot volcanic springs in the area, which can be savoured by both scuba divers and snorkellers – and, for those who want to stay dry, from a glass-bottom boat.

The forest and mangroves are a haven for birdlife

Dominica

The volcanic, rainforested island of Dominica thrusts out of the Caribbean Sea from a deep magical underwater seascape of submerged pinnacles and corals.

On land, Dominica offers nature in the raw, divided by a cloud-covered spine of forested peaks, narrow ridges, bubbling waterfalls, sulphurous springs and a boiling lake. Wild and untamed, this 'Nature Island' is the only Caribbean island that Christopher Columbus would still be able to recognise some 500 years later.

In the Windward Islands, between French Guadeloupe and Martinique, Dominica has been settled by Britain and France. English is the official language, but a French Creole patois is widely spoken. The island remains the last outpost of the Carib Indians (Kalingo), Amerindians who were calling the Caribbean home centuries before the Europeans arrived. The blending of the Carib, African, French and English cultures is celebrated on Creole Day at the end of October or in the beginning of November, when everyone wears national costume to go to work or school.

Cocoa and coffee-growing under the French gave way to the cultivation of sugar and limes under the British. Bananas became the byword for economic success in the 1930s, but with plantation economies in decline, Dominica turned to eco-tourism. Indicative of this emphasis is the latest tourist attraction to be completed, the **Waitukubuli National Trail**, which runs 115 miles (184km) from the far north to the far south, touching both east and west coasts, up and down mountains, across rivers and through forest reserves – a hiker's dream.

Natural Wonders

Dominica has two cruise ship terminals: Portsmouth, the northern port, is the perfect starting point for a boat ride along Indian River, for scenic wanderings in the Cabrits National Park, or for a trip into Carib Territory. Roseau, the island's capital, in the south, offers an even wider range of options, from a Jeep safari into the tropical interior to a trek to the Valley of Desolation and Boiling Lake.

Most cruise lines focus on trips (by minibus or Jeep) to the Emerald Pool, Titou Gorge or Trafalgar Falls, but you can go independently by taxi, too. You can also go on kayak, canyoning, scuba-diving and snorkelling trips, as well as whale-watching safaris off the west coast.

Under the Sea

Part of Dominica's appeal is the sharpness with which the ocean floor drops off from the shore, reaching depths of several hundred metres. Most shore excursions include the option of exploring the reefs or snorkelling in the shallows.

Carib craftsman

Scuba-diving is mostly around Soufrière Bay and Scotts Head, where hot and cold water springs bubble under the surface. But diving is also feasible in the north, around the Cabrits Peninsula – and at night, when octopuses, turtles, stingrays and the black-tipped reef sharks reveal themselves.

Roseau

Tatty tin-roofed houses and old French colonial buildings with hanging verandas give **Roseau** (pronounced Ro-zo) a ramshackle air. Dominicans are dedicated to the land and most have their own vegetable 'gardens' either up in the forest or next to their home. Saturday is market day when the bounty of the countryside is brought into town.

A T-shaped cruise ship pier allows you to disembark on Bayfront in the middle of town for some sightseeing followed by a meal at the historic Fort Young, now a waterfront hotel.

Trafalgar Falls

The engaging **Dominica Museum** (Mon–Fri 9am–4pm, Sat 9am–noon; charge), is housed in the old post office, and covers everything from island geology and economy to the history of the slave trade. Behind it is the Old Market Plaza, still used by vendors of crafts and souvenirs, containing the old, red market cross. A walk up King George V Street will lead you to the **Botanical Gardens**, the main recreational park, used for cultural events. In 1979, Hurricane David devastated the vegetation, leaving uprooted trees still visible, including an African baobab tree. There is still a varied collection of tropical trees, however, proof that everything in Dominica grows at a rapid rate.

> ### Carib ancestors
>
> South American Indians from the Orinoco River region are likely to be the ancestors of the 3,000 Caribs/Kalinago who continue to survive in Dominica on fishing, weaving, carving, and basket-making.

Trafalgar Falls

Most cruise lines offer a Jeep safari into the rainforest and to **Trafalgar Falls** (daily; charge), or you can take a taxi. From the capital you cross a valley that was once a productive lime and cocoa plantation. Kalabash trees, bananas, avocados and mangoes line the winding roads. Beyond are orchids, heliconia and the red-flowering ginger lily, as well as the cinnamon tree.

The short trail to the waterfalls is signalled by a handy bar and restaurant and craft vendors round the car park. An invigorating but comfortable climb through dense vegetation ends in a viewing platform overlooking two waterfalls. Keen swimmers can clamber over slippery rocks to bathe in the pool, but swimming is better at the **Titou Gorge**, where hot and cold streams intermingle in a natural plunge pool.

The Boiling Lake

One of the toughest trails in the Caribbean, the hike to the **Boiling Lake** is used as a fitness test by the Dominican army, and is offered only by cruise lines with a fair proportion of active passengers. This full-day hike from the Titou Gorge up into the **Morne Trois Pitons National Park**, a UNESCO World Heritage Site, takes up to four hours in each direction. Rewards include the pleasures of passing under canopies of greenery formed by giant tree ferns, of fording mineral-rich streams, relishing rare views of Martinique and Guadeloupe, and climbing knife-edged ridges into a primeval landscape.

The track passes through the **Valley of Desolation**, a lunar landscape in a long, jagged volcanic fissure, with boiling pools of mud and vents and geysers belching out stinking clouds of sulphurous gases.

Suddenly the Boiling Lake comes into view, it is usually shrouded in clouds of steam. When the mists clear, the magma-heated cauldron reveals a surface heaving with bub-

Whale Watching

Dominica is the ideal place to spot pilot whales, false-killer whales, sperm whales and spotted whales, as well as bottle-nosed dolphins. Between November and March, a classic whale and dolphin trip offers a 90 percent success rate in spotting both creatures. The catamarans are equipped with sonar, backed up by a look-out scanning the surface for tell-tale signs. The boats head along the west coast, stopping regularly to take soundings. The humpback whale is more often heard than seen, and you may see one just basking at the surface, like a huge rock, until after about 40 minutes or so it flips its great black fin tail and dives back down into the depths. The pilot whale prefers to travel in pods of 60, while a sperm whale might be accompanied by a 6-metre (20ft) calf. As for dolphins, they love to surf the wake of the boat.

bles – the second largest pot of boiling water in the world.

Portsmouth

Smaller cruise ships sometimes dock in to **Portsmouth**, within easy reach of **Cabrits National Park**, a spectacular dry tropical forest full of bay, mahogany, sandbox, white cedar and logwood. Among the trees are the lovingly restored 18th-century British fortifications of **Fort Shirley** (daily; charge), complete with gun batteries, storehouses and officers' quarters. It is a moving sight to see small cruise ships under sail come

Valley of Desolation

into Prince Rupert Bay and anchor just under the fortress, much as ships must have done since the 18th century when it was built. The seascape around the headland is a protected marine park providing excellent diving and snorkelling.

South of town, a popular excursion is to travel by wooden boat along the **Indian River**, festooned with foliage, and the boatmen will point out the wildlife as you go. There's no need to book in advance as enterprising boatmen will be vying to take you.

From Portsmouth you can also take a trip to the **Carib Territory** along the northeastern wild Atlantic coast, where Dominica's Carib/Kalinago Indians grow cassava (manioc), live in houses built on stilts and sell colourful basketwork from stalls by the roadside. In the Carib Territory is a model village, **Kalinago Barana Auté** (tours; charge; www.kalinago baranaaute.com), where guides explain the culture and history of the people and you can watch women weaving their intricate and beautiful baskets, before a singing and dancing folklore troupe bids visitors a traditional farewell.

Martinique

As with Guadeloupe, arriving in Martinique is like taking a big step into France spiked with a large dose of Caribbean flavour. Strange as it may seem, disembarking here means that you are entering the French Republic and visiting a far-flung corner of the European Union, where the local currency is the euro, and the people speak French.

It may not feel much like it to begin with, but this Caribbean island is politically and constitutionally a part of

The coastline of Martinique

France. Since 1946, when its people voted to become an overseas *département*, Martinique, like Guadeloupe, has been a little, tropical piece of Europe. Its people are French citizens, enjoying the same rights as any other *citoyens*, and in many ways act just like their European

Diamond Rock

The Rocher du Diamant (Diamond Rock), off the south coast, an outcrop off volcanic stone jutting from the sea, was occupied by the British for 18 months in 1805–6 and renamed HMS *Diamond*.

compatriots, but with one major exception – they are also Caribbean.

As you travel about the island you will notice how French it is, compared with other islands – the well-maintained roads, signs and industrial zones and the villages and towns with their churches, squares and town halls. But the difference is that they are located around a bay, edged with black beaches the further north you go, and white beaches to the south. The church and square lead on to a promenade and jetty jutting out into the bay, where each fishing community hauls in their catch and sells it in the beachside pavilions. Here you can hear the locals discussing the state of the world in Créole, a French-based patois.

Fort-de-France

Cruise ships arrive in **Fort-de-France**, the island's main port and capital, a city of more than 200,000 inhabitants. Some dock at Quai des Tourelles, to the east of the old city, by the naval dockyard. From here, it is a short taxi ride into the centre, or a long, hot walk. If you are lucky your ship will berth at the purpose-built **Pointe Simon Terminal**, close to the heart of the city. In a matter of minutes you can be in the bustling and unmistakably French-flavoured shopping streets of the capital. There is little to keep you at the cruise terminal and it is better to head straight out on to boulevard Alfassa, the road running parallel to the waterfront, where you'll find plenty of public minibuses to take you to different parts of the island.

Like most Caribbean ports, Fort-de-France has had its fair share of fires, earthquakes and other natural disasters, so there are many modern structures among the more interesting 19th-century (and earlier) buildings. What hasn't changed, however, is the grid of narrow streets, which are constantly jammed with traffic. Numerous small boutiques selling the latest Paris fashions are tucked between shabby shops offering local crafts and commodities. Crossing the pedestrianised rue de la République and rue Victor Schoelcher (named after an anti-slavery campaigner) is rue Victor Hugo, where a couple of small shopping malls offer an impressive array of designer perfumes and clothing. Further up

Fruit market in Fort-de-France

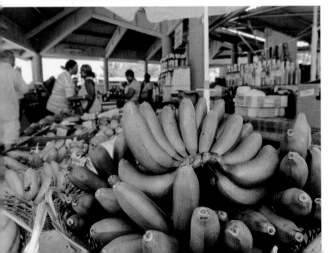

rue de la République you reach a square and a much larger shopping mall, Cour Perrinon, with a car park.

Restaurants and Markets

The centre of Fort-de-France can be explored comfortably on foot in a few hours, and there will still be time for a leisurely meal at one of the city's many excellent restaurants (try the delicious *accras*, deep-fried fritters stuffed with prawns or salted cod).

> ### Empress Joséphine
>
> The Empress Joséphine, Napoléon Bonaparte's first wife, was born in Martinique in 1763. It is believed she was behind her husband's decision to reinstate slavery in 1802, after it had been abolished during the French Revolution. A statue of her in La Savane was decapitated in an apparent symbolic act of vandalism in 1991.

But no French town would be worth its salt if it didn't have a market or two, and Fort-de-France has its share. The busy open-air markets, which operate all day every day, are most colourful on Friday and Saturday. The fish market takes place from early in the morning until dusk on the banks of the Rivière Madame, a 15-minute walk north of the Pointe Simon terminal. The nearest market to the port, the Grand Marché, has a few vegetable stalls and vendors in Martinican dress mostly selling crafts, spices and souvenirs.

Metal Landmarks

Occasional buildings stand out as a reminder of Martinique's long French history. Some houses have ornate gingerbread fretwork, a style imported from Louisiana in the 19th century, intricate wrought-ironwork and pretty pastel colours. Most eye-catching, perhaps, are two buildings credited to the architect Henri Picq, a contemporary of Gustave Eiffel and, some claim, the true designer of the Eiffel Tower. The Romanesque-style **St Louis Cathedral**, on rue Schoelcher, hints at the architect's love affair with metal girders and joists, its steel-reinforced spire rising 60 metres (200ft) into the sky. Built in 1895 to withstand any earthquake, this strange blend of tradition and innovation, known as the 'iron cathedral', has a cool interior and fine stained-glass windows.

A couple of streets further east stands Pick's other lasting contribution to the capital's exotic architectural heritage. The imposing library, the **Bibliothèque Schoelcher** (Mon 1–5.30pm, Tue–Fri 8.30am–5.30pm, Sat 8.30am–noon), is a spectacular blend of Romanesque, Byzantine and Egyptian influences, again dominated by prefabricated cast-iron and steel features. With ornate gables, a large glass dome and coloured metal panels, this is a truly unique building, lit up at night, and decorated with clusters of French flags and exotic tropical trees.

Out of the windows you can see Fort-de-France's 'green lung', the large expanse of grass, palms and tamarind trees known as **La Savane** that contains the city centre to the east. Traditionally the place for sitting, gossiping and whiling the hours away, you can browse through the collections of T-shirts and mass-produced Haitian-style paintings in the covered craft market opposite the waterfront or just sit on one of the benches and watch the coming and going of local ferries that set off from the nearby pier. Also in the gardens is a statue of Pierre Belain d'Esnambuc, who claimed the island for France in 1635 and founded the original fort in St Pierre.

Alternatively, have a drink at one of the hotels or restaurants along the rue de la Liberté, next to La Savane.

Ferry tickets

Two companies run ferries between Fort-de-France and Trois Ilets, 15 minutes away to the south. Buy a single ticket so that you can return on either ferry, otherwise you might find yourself having to pay twice for the journey.

Fort St Louis

As you sail into Fort-de-France, you cannot miss the impressive bulk of **Fort St Louis**. The citadel has been continuously occupied by the French military since the mid-17th century and is still an active naval base, but parts of it can be visited. One interesting feature is its unusually low ceilings, reputedly designed to deter attacks from taller British troops in the era of inter-European rivalry.

St-Pierre

Martinique is not a large island, but it is clearly impossible to see everything in the space of a few hours in port.

Les Anses d'Arlet

Most cruise ship excursions involve a trip to a rum distillery, to some beautiful botanical gardens or to the historic town of St-Pierre, victim of the 20th-century's worst volcanic disaster. All these are definitely worth doing, although the expedition to St-Pierre takes an hour each way.

Perhaps the most evocative site in Martinique is the town of **St-Pierre**, situated on the northwest coast under the brooding volcano, Montagne Pelée. In May 1902, this volcano erupted, killing all but one – he had been thrown in jail the night before for drunkenness – of the town's 30,000 inhabitants and devastating what was known as the 'Paris of the Antilles'. Many of the ruins of this sophisticated and fun-loving place, such as its grand theatre and main church, lie

The bell of St-Pierre Cathedral on display

just as they have for more than a century. A new town has grown up through the rubble of the old, with cafés and restaurants along the black sand beach and smart promenade, to refresh the curious visitor. There is a restored covered market on the waterfront and the local tourist office organises fascinating tours of the historic ruins. The **Musée Vulcanologique** (daily 9am–5pm; charge) has graphic images and artefacts – such as a church bell twisted by the heat of the volcano *(see above)* – from before and after the cataclysm and explains how modern science has made a repetition of the disaster impossible.

Rum and Gardens

Martinique is dotted with sugar plantations and rum distilleries, producing the world-famous *rhum agricole*, a white rum made from sugar cane juice rather than molasses. Most are open for free visits, but you will be encouraged to taste (and buy) some of the potent liquor. The **Distillerie Depaz** (Mon–Sat 9am–5pm), north of St-Pierre, offers a well-marked trail through each stage of rum manufacturing.

Those more interested in tropical flora should take a tour to the **Jardin de Balata** (daily 9am–6pm, last entry 4.30pm; charge; www.jardindebalata.fr), on the steep, twisting **Route de la Trace**, which cuts through the rainforested mountains north of Fort-de-France to Le Morne Rouge. At their best after the rainy season at the end of the year, these gardens have a stunning collection of flowers, exotic trees and shrubs. Nearby, the **Eglise de Sacré Coeur** is a smaller but almost exact replica of the Parisian original, standing among tropical foliage with spectacular mountain views.

St Lucia

Sandwiched between Martinique and St Vincent, St Lucia (pronounced *Loo-sha*) is the largest of the Windward Islands at 43km (27 miles) long and 22km (14 miles) wide. With a calm Caribbean coastline acting as a counterpoint to the wind-buffeted Atlantic shore, the mango-shaped island is seductively lush and has preserved its green mountainous heart with banana plantations giving way to vibrant forests. The south is dominated by the Pitons, the jungle-clad twin peaks that symbolise St Lucia.

The Pitons mountains at sunset

A Cultural Mélange

Culturally, the island is an engaging mix, with Caribbean flair, Creole artlessness and French finesse underscored by traditional British values. The island has changed hands 14 times, with the French and British flags alternating from 1650, when French settlers first landed. From the 1760s the island operated a plantation economy, based on African slave labour. St Lucia became British for good in 1814; it gained independence in 1979 but remains part of the Commonwealth. English is the official language but Kwéyòl (Creole patois) is commonplace – French and English vocabulary imposed on African grammar. St Lucia feels safe but wild, forthright yet not as in-your-face as Jamaica, as friendly as Barbados but less primly British.

Until recently, agriculture, chiefly bananas, was the mainstay of the economy, but the island is making a successful transition to tourism. St Lucia now has a variety of luxurious hotels, mid-range all-inclusive resorts and low-key traditional inns for those who wish to stay on.

Castries

As a port of call, **Castries** is perfectly suited to the largest cruise ships, which dock at the **Pointe Seraphine Cruise Terminal** on the north side of the harbour or at **La Place Carenage**, Queen Elizabeth II dock, on the south side. Both sides have information bureaux, communications centres and duty-free shops. A variety of excursions are also available in air-conditioned minibuses.

Taxi minder

Taxis in Castries are well organised with an official 'minder' at the taxi rank who establishes routes, states prices and helps form small groups to visit places together. Prices are standardised for set routes but you can check at the tourist office booth close by.

Kayaking in St Lucia

Taxis queue up offering guided trips to those who prefer to look around on their own, but it's important to remember that the ship will not wait for you.

Water taxis ply the harbour between Pointe Seraphine and La Place Carenage. The latter is right by the Vendors' Arcade and the Central Market, which is busiest on Friday or Saturday. Many old colonial buildings were destroyed in fires in 1927 and 1948 but the iron market survived, as did houses on Brazil Street and the Roman Catholic cathedral containing paintings by St Lucian artist, Dunstan St Omer.

Literary Hero

The main square in Castries was renamed **Derek Walcott Square** in 1993, in honour of the St Lucian poet who won the Nobel Prize for literature. The square is shaded by a huge, 400-year-old Saman tree known locally as a *massair*; the story goes that a foreigner once asked the name of the tree and was told *massair*, which simply means 'I don't know' in Kwéyòl.

On top of the hill to the south of the town is the **Morne Fortune Historic Area** where, along with some remarkable views, you will find the old military buildings of Fort Charlotte, originally built by the French in 1768 and completed by the British in 1814.

Southwest to the Pitons

If you head southwest and inland from town through the hills, you will come to banana plantations in **Cul de Sac Valley**. St Lucians claim that the volcanic soil makes their bananas the sweetest, juiciest ones on earth. The blue plastic bags you see covering them help retain moisture and protect them from insects and too much sun, reducing the need for chemicals. The west coast road twists and turns southwards to the lovely fishing village of **Anse la Raye**, where trinket-sellers and fishermen cluster around the beachfront.

From here, the road skirts the lush rainforest giving glimpses of the dramatic **Pitons**, the twin cones which tower over the trees. **Gros Piton** rises more than 774 metres (2,540ft) above the sea, while **Petit Piton** stands 716 metres (2,350ft) high.

The peaks have always had a certain mystique: the Amerindians left sacred carvings on the rock, believing that the Petit Piton, the 'small' peak that dwarfs Soufrière, was giving birth to a baby.

In the rainforest, mahogany and red cedars grow, as well as the gommier trees where the island parrots live. This part of the island was badly hit by Hurricane Tomas in 2010 and, while the road is now open, gashes can still be seen on the mountainsides where there were mudslides.

The town of Soufrière

Soufrière

The quaintly ramshackle town of **Soufrière** nestles under the twin peaks and marks the gateway to a fascinating 3-hectare (7-acre) volcanic crater, **La Soufrière Sulphur Springs** (daily 9am–5pm; charge). No longer active, the volcano's sulphurous vapours are believed by some to have a positive effect on the sinuses and the springs to have therapeutic value. However, most visitors are overwhelmed by the rotten egg-like smell of the sulphur. The crater, which collapsed about 40,000 years ago, has bubbling pools of lava that steam away like an inferno.

Diamond Falls

Nearby are the beautifully maintained **Diamond Botanical Gardens, Mineral Baths and Waterfall** (Mon–Sat 10am–5pm, Sun 10am–3pm; charge). The gardens were created in 1785, just before the French Revolution, with funds provided by Louis XVI. While it is considered unsafe to swim in the volcanic falls, bathing in the rejuvenating mineral baths, fed by hot springs, is permissible. Among the foliage and primary colours in the garden are bold red and yellow crab's claw, ginger lily, rare orchids, trailing red heliconia, mimosa, poinsettia, and over 140 types of ferns.

Sailing and Snorkelling

An alternative way to explore the west coast is by sea, organised through the cruise line or at the marina in Castries. Boat tours can include a spot of diving, snorkelling, swimming or sport fishing. **Anse Chastanet**, just north of Soufrière, is the best place for snorkelling and diving, as its reef is in a national marine park. Halfway along the west coast lies **Marigot Bay**, a magnificent steep-sided cove. The picturesque bay is full of yachts at harbour and there are several hotels and restaurants on the waterfront.

The spectacular volcanic Diamond Falls

Rodney Bay

To the north of Castries lie sheltered bays, beautiful beaches, hotels, a marina, historic landmarks and shopping malls. **Rodney Bay** is the main resort area, where **Reduit Beach** is one of the best stretches of sand on the island. Plenty of water sports are offered here and it is a pleasant place to spend the day. Shopping is good in the new Baywalk Mall at the junction of the main highway and Reduit Beach Road, with designer outlets, a supermarket and also a casino. The road is lined with restaurants, bars, cafés and ice cream parlours, as well as banks, ATMs, tour operators and cybercafés.

Further along the highway you get to the huge entrance of the **Rodney Bay Marina** with more restaurants and bars. This is also the finishing point of an annual sailing event, the Atlantic Rally for Cruisers.

At the far northern end of Rodney Bay lies the **Pigeon Island National Landmark** (daily 9am–5pm; interpretative centre closed on Sun; charge) and the ruins of Fort Rodney, where there is another good beach. Once used as a lookout post during the European tugs of war, the park is now the main venue for the **St Lucia Jazz Festival** every May. Kayaking trips can be arranged around Pigeon Island.

Yes, We Have No Bananas…

Bananas have been the backbone of the St Lucian economy since the 1950s. They are a perfect crop for the small farmer as they only take six months to grow, are happy on steep hillsides and fruit all year round. However, the survival of Caribbean banana growers is under threat due to a World Trade Organisation ruling that they must compete with massive US-backed Latin American companies. The Caribbean growers had enjoyed preferential treatment from the EU, which helped keep the small island economies afloat, but the US complained that it was unfair and illegal.

Now the surviving plantations depend entirely on exports to Britain where many consumers will pay more for fruit grown with fewer chemicals, on farms where the labour is fairly paid. Visit www.cbea.org.

A Day of Adventure

Active shore excursions include an aerial tram ride through the rainforest canopy followed by zip-lining through the trees, a jungle bike ride, ATV tours or jeep safaris. One of the best routes heads south to the waterfall close to Anse la Raye and visits the restored 18th-century **Sikwi Sugar Mill**. Golfers can prebook to play at the **Cap Estate Country Club** or at **Sandals St Lucia**.

Barbados

The most easterly of the Windward Islands, Barbados is a coral island, not volcanic like most of its neighbours with dramatic mountains and lush rainforests. Instead, it has open, rolling countryside with fields of sugar cane rippling in the breezes that come in off the Atlantic, which crashes in huge rollers onto the sweeping beaches of the exposed east coast.

Outside the busy capital Bridgetown, the 430-sq km (166-sq mile) island is dotted with sleepy villages and beautiful botanical gardens and plantation houses. The chattel houses, wooden shacks that were once home to plantation workers, have become an architectural feature. Painted in primary colours and pastel shades, with intricate fretwork around the windows, they often double as craft shops.

At the beach in Barbados

The sheltered west coast is lined with some of the Caribbean's most glamorous and expensive hotels, whose patrons return year after year. The island has gained a reputation as a millionaire's hideaway, particularly thanks to US$1,500-a-night establishments like Sandy Lane, and several smart, exclusive restaurants.

Although it is increasingly influenced by the US, Barbados has a distinctly British feel, with cricket played on village greens and red post boxes. The island was settled by the British in the 17th century and is still a member of the Common-

Calypso fever

Crop Over starts at the end of June with Pic-o-de-Crop calypso competitions and culminates in a massive Kadooment Day parade on the first Monday in August. This is when politicians can find themselves at the sharp end of the calypso songwriters' pens.

wealth. It is clean, friendly and regarded as safe, although the usual issues of extreme wealth flaunted in the face of relative poverty exist.

Despite years of colonialism, Barbados has its own colourful heritage; its annual Crop Over festival held in the summer, celebrating the sugar cane harvest, is rated as one of the best events in the Caribbean.

The jazz festival in January attracts big names such as Patti LaBelle and Ellis Marsalis, while Holders' Season in March, a wonderful series of outdoor classical music performances on a former plantation estate, has drawn performers, including the London Symphony Orchestra.

A Turnaround Port

With ships calling daily during the high-season winter months, Barbados is one of the Caribbean islands' most visited by cruise passengers. Apart from an added gleam in the eyes of the shopkeepers, a cruise ship in town does not make a vast difference to daily life, since locals are used to tourists and the island has a well-developed infrastructure, and the many visitor attractions are well distributed.

Many cruise lines start and finish cruises here, particularly those carrying a high proportion of passengers from Europe, since the island is well served by non-stop international flights. In fact some 665,000 cruise ship passengers visited Barbados in 2010.

It is one of the easiest destinations in which to stay on after a cruise – well worth doing, if only to sample the nightlife, which varies from fine cuisine under the stars at The Cliff restaurant to dancing all night long at a beachfront nightclub on the south coast.

 The cruise terminal is about 2km (1 mile) from the centre of **Bridgetown**, at the **Deep Water Harbour**. It has a duty-free shopping centre for jewellery, cameras and electrical goods (which are still more expensive than in the US or Europe), as well as souvenir stalls selling T-shirts. You need a passport, airline ticket or cruise line ID to qualify for duty-free prices. Visitors can also hire bikes and arrange tours at the terminal. Cars

Palm-fringed Crane beach

are available to rent just outside the terminal building; you will need your driving licence from home and Bds$10 for a local drivers' permit.

Other facilities include an internet café, sports bar and restaurant. **Brighton Beach** is right next to the port, where you can relax if you don't want to explore, but keep an eye on your valuables. There's a popular bar here too, **Weisers**, and games of volleyball are played on the beach every afternoon.

Rum in the Sun

Cockspur (formerly Malibu) Beach Club (Mon–Fri 9am–5pm; no tours 11am–noon, last tour 3.45pm; charge; tel: 425 9393), also on Brighton Beach, offers tours of the West Indies Rum Distillery here, lunch, beach chairs and water sports. Close by on Spring Garden Highway, is the **Mount Gay** rum blending and bottling plant (Mon–Fri 9am–5pm, Sat 10am–4pm; tours every hour, 9.30am–3.30pm; charge; tel: 425 8757), which operates comprehensive 45-minute tours, including a tasting of one of the local favourite rums.

Getting Around Barbados

Barbados is quite an easy island to explore independently and is only 34km (21 miles) long, although twisting country roads make distances seem further, especially when the sugar cane is high and views are obscured. Shore excursions involve many permutations of the island tour and are usually comprehensive, but the fun of exploring is lost if you travel by coach. An open-sided Mini Moke is a better way to get around, and in a day trip from Bridgetown you should be able to get to the north and return via the wild scenery of the Atlantic coast.

Driving is on the left, and rush hour starts at 4pm. However, while all roads lead to Bridgetown, progress may be extremely slow around this time (nobody is in much of a hurry on Barbados anyway), so do allow for this – and also for getting lost, as the country roads are not well signposted.

Taxis are plentiful and line up outside the cruise terminal. Drivers are more than willing to do day trips. Fares are supposed to be fixed but there is no meter system, so always agree a price in advance. The island has a comprehensive bus network and the single flat fare is a bargain, but again, journeys can take a considerable time.

Bridgetown

If you have only a few hours, there is plenty to see and do without leaving **Bridgetown**. The road into Bridgetown leads down to the **Careenage**, lined with yachts and fishing boats. This is where ships used to have their hulls repaired or cleaned. Alongside is the restored Old Spirit Bond warehouse, which houses the **Verandah Art Gallery** (Mon–Fri 9am–4pm, Sat 9am–1pm; tel: 426 2605) that has good exhibitions of Caribbean art. Across the pedestrianised Chamberlain Bridge, which was once a swing bridge, and through Independence Arch, is the **Waterfront Café**, where you can enjoy a lazy lunch with tasty local specialities and a good view.

National Heroes

Walking in Bridgetown

Back across the bridge is **National Heroes Square** (formerly Trafalgar Square) dedicated to 10 Barbadian heroes – but no longer to Lord Nelson whose statue still stands in the centre and will be relocated one day.

At the northern end of the square the Gothic-style Parliament building dates back to 1872, while nearby **St**

The Careenage in Bridgetown

Michael's Cathedral stands on the grounds of the first church in Barbados, which was built in 1665.

Broad Street, off to the left of Heroes Square, is the main shopping area. Cave Shepherd and Harrison's are the principal Bajan department stores; if you don't have time to leave town to shop, look out for the beautifully crafted pottery from Earthworks, which is on sale in Cave Shepherd. The Best of Barbados gift shops are a good bet for locally made souvenirs – everything on sale is produced on the island.

Driving from Bridgetown to the south coast you reach the **Garrison Savannah**, dating from the mid-17th century and once the most important military location on the island *(see page 146)*. The area is packed with historic interest, with forts, monuments, military buildings and the world's largest collection of 17th-century cannons (tel: 430 0900 for a tour). The **Barbados Museum** (Mon–Sat 9am–5pm, Sun 2–6pm; charge; www.barbmuse.org.bb) is also here, displaying everything from Amerindian artefacts to colonial furniture, and rare historical maps of the island.

The Platinum Coast

The west coast, dubbed the **Platinum Coast**, is lined with smart hotels and exclusive villas hidden by trees and iron gates. Drive up Highway 1 and you'll see that Bajan life continues regardless, among the holiday paradises. There are several public paths down to the soft white sand and you can swim from the beach in front of the **Sandy Lane Hotel** – no one can own a beach in Barbados.

Holetown is where the first settlers landed in 1627, an event which is commemorated every February with street fairs, concerts and a music festival. There is a wide choice of restaurants and branches of the main Bridgetown stores in the shopping centre, plus gift shops in the Chattel Village.

Nearby, **Folkestone Marine Park and Visitors Centre** (Mon–Fri 9am–5pm, Sat–Sun 10am–6pm; charge) has an un-

Cricket, Lovely Cricket...

Barbadians are passionate about cricket – it's their national game. When the West Indies are playing at the Kensington Oval, within walking distance of the port, everyone tunes in to their radios, especially if the opponents are their old colonial masters, and a carnival atmosphere prevails. However, the West Indies team has been experiencing a downturn in its fortunes during this millennium and its international ranking has fallen from its heyday in the 1960s to early 1990s.

Cricket was introduced to the West Indies by the British military more than 200 years ago to encourage community spirit. Since then Barbados has produced a long line of brilliant players, and hosted some of the matches in the World Cup in 2007. Contact the Barbados Cricket Association, tel: 436 1397; www.bcacricket.org.

derwater snorkel trail over a 11km (7-mile) coral reef (glass-bottom boats for non-swimmers) as well as changing facilities.

Speightstown

If you're in need of some solid ground beneath your feet, take a guided hike along the **Arbib Nature and Heritage Trail** (Wed, Thur, Sat; tel: 426 2421), which starts at St Peter's Church in **Speightstown**, once a thriving port shipping sugar to

Wild green monkey

England. Twinned with Charleston, South Carolina, Speightstown has a faded charm with two-storey, balconied 'shop houses' typical of an early Barbadian town dwelling, with the business premises on the ground floor and living quarters above. The restored 17th-century **Arlington House** (daily 9am–5pm; charge) is a fine example, and has a museum showing Barbados' early connections with the Carolinas.

Further north, the landscape becomes flatter and more desolate with remote beaches, rocky cliffs and pounding waves. Cut across to see the green monkeys and tortoises at the well laid out **Barbados Wildlife Reserve** and for a forest walk with fantastic views at **Grenade Hall Forest and Signal Station** (daily 10am–5pm; charge covers both).

Further on, you can look round **St Nicholas Abbey** (Sun–Fri 10am–3.30pm; charge), a 17th-century Jacobean mansion and one of the oldest houses on the island, where they make their own rum. A worthwhile detour is to **Morgan Lewis Mill** (Mon–Sat 9am–5pm; charge; tel: 426 2421) in St

Washington's home

George Washington spent two months in Barbados in 1751, when he was 19. The house where he stayed, by the Garrison Savannah, has been restored and is open to visitors (Mon–Fri 10am–4pm; charge).

Andrew. Restored by the Barbados National Trust, it is the island's only working windmill.

The Wild East Coast

Approaching the east coast from the north, you can see miles of Atlantic rollers and craggy limestone coral cliffs all the way to **Bathsheba**, an authentic village unscathed by time and popular with surfers. It is not safe to swim in the sea here but you can cool off in the many rock pools before enjoying a good Barbadian buffet at **Bonito's Bar and Restaurant** on the shore or at the **Atlantis Hotel** in Tent Bay.

As you leave Bathsheba, the **Andromeda Botanic Gardens** (daily 9am–5pm; charge) is a wonderful place for a rest from driving. Waterfalls splash gently through the gardens, dazzling with tropical blooms from all over the Caribbean.

Natural Wonders

In the heart of the island are three fascinating examples of natural Barbados. The **Flower Forest** in St Joseph (daily; charge; tel: 433 8152) is a pretty walking trail through lush tropical gardens. **Welchman Hall Gully** (daily 9am–4.30pm; charge) is a deep ravine just off Highway 2, maintained by the National Trust, with a trail leading through rainforest. Look out for green monkeys and colourful birds in the trees.

Close by is **Harrison's Cave** (daily; first tour 8.30am, last tour 3.45pm; charge), a vast limestone cave complete with underground lakes, cascading water, stalactites and stalagmites, all of which can be seen from a small electric train that carries passengers through the cave network.

Sporting Chances

There are plenty of activities on offer in Barbados. The island is awash with golf courses and if you book far enough in advance you can play at the prestigious course at **Sandy Lane** (tel: 444 2000) or at the public **Barbados Golf Club** (tel: 428 8463) in the south, also a championship golf course.

Horseriding, biking and hiking in the central highlands is a good way to feel the essence of the countryside, and as for the sea, there is windsurfing, best on the east coast in the winter months, and sailing off the south coast beaches, and the waves at the magnificent **Crane Beach** in the southeast are perfect for body boarding. Afterwards you can relax with a rum punch on the Crane Hotel's wonderful clifftop terrace.

Harrison's Cave

THE SOUTHERN CARIBBEAN

Cruising further south, it is mainly the smaller cruise and sailing ships that call at the 30-odd coral islands collectively known as the Grenadines, many of which are tinier than some of the ships. The diving and snorkelling in this part of the Caribbean are exemplary and the idyllic beaches and lagoons practically a cliché. The islands, off the Venezuelan coast, offer a fascinating mix of cultures and landscapes from South

American jungle in Trinidad to desert in Aruba.

St Vincent and The Grenadines

At 30 by 18km (18 by 11 miles), **St Vincent** is the largest and most developed of the Grenadines, remaining relatively unspoilt, it lies between St Lucia and Grenada and 160km (100 miles) west of Barbados. At **Kingstown**, the island port and capital, there are berths for two ships, linked to a cruise terminal, so it is rare that ships have to anchor offshore and tender passengers to land as they do at the other Grenadine islands, such as Bequia and Mayreau.

Clear waters of the Grenadines

Built in 2001, the terminal has more stores, cafés, bars and fast food outlets than the town centre, where the street hawkers and shops mainly serve local needs. An indoor fruit and vegetable market (Upper Bay) and a covered fish market, known as Little Tokyo, by the dock, provide some colour.

Kingstown's Catholic **Cathedral of the Assumption** is a bizarre mixture of Moorish, Romanesque, Byzantine, Venetian and Flemish architectural styles, despite being built in the 1930s. An 18th-century fortress, **Fort Charlotte**, which stands guard above the town, has some spectacular views.

Outside Kingstown

There are plenty of taxis waiting outside the terminal, all keen to offer guided tours around the island and, if two or more of you are travelling together, a taxi tour is cheaper than a ship excursion. Alternatively, minibuses heading to specific places leave regularly from the fish market. St Vincent is a lush, forested island, and this is evident in the **Botanic Gardens** in Montrose (daily 7am–6pm), a five- or 10-minute drive from the port. Established in 1765, they are believed to be the oldest in the Western Hemisphere and have a breadfruit tree that dates back to the original plant brought to the island by Captain Bligh, of *Mutiny on the Bounty* fame.

Another way of seeing St Vincent is by boat from Kingstown along the Caribbean coast, past sugar and banana plantations, a former whaling village, rocky coves, black sand beaches and mountains, including the Soufrière volcano which last erupted in 1979, and round to the **Falls of Baleine**, where you can swim in the rock-enclosed freshwater pool created by the waterfall.

La Soufrière

The great advantage of visiting St Vincent is the scope for walking tours – from gentle nature hikes right up to a strenuous ascent of the 1,178-metre (3,864ft) **La Soufrière**. The latter, however, will take a full day, including getting from Kingstown to the volcano in the island's northeast corner; whether this is feasible depends on your fitness and walking experience, the

Hanging heliconia

Walking up to La Soufrière

weather and the departure time of your ship.

Check with the tourist office in the terminal, where it is also possible to hire a guide. For an easier option, try the **Vermont Nature Trails**, through rainforest in the Buccament Valley, about a 20-minute drive away. Or you can take a Jeep safari tour.

Bequia and Mayreau

While St Vincent remains a real haven for nature-lovers, more cruise ships are choosing to call at **Bequia** and Mayreau. **Port Elizabeth** is the entry point for Bequia although only the smallest cruise ships – often sailing vessels – call here, they all have to anchor in Admiralty Bay.

Once on the jetty (where the ferries from St Vincent also disembark), it is only a short walk to a group of smart shops and restaurants, and a tourist information office. There are more places to shop and eat along the harbour front (Belmont Walkway), or you could head inland for a few minutes along Front Street, where you will find an open-air market.

A Water Heaven

An attractive island, Bequia is really about the water. Snorkelling and scuba diving are the main reasons for coming here, and there are plenty of water taxis to get you around. The best diving sites are within the 12km (7-mile) coral reef, which has been designated a national marine park. You can also travel by boat from the main jetty to the nearest beach. And – unlike on volcanic St Vincent – the beaches are all golden sand.

Mayreau is just 2.6 sq km (1 sq mile) of beautiful beaches and palm trees. In the past cotton and cocoa have been grown on the island. Only small cruise ships can anchor here and passengers are tendered to **Saline Bay Beach** or **Salt Whistle Bay** for a relaxing day swimming and snorkelling.

Other Grenadine islands at which some ships call include the five uninhabited islets of **Tobago Cays**, protected by a large reef; the idyllic resort of **Palm Island**; **Canouan**, with Donald Trump's championship golf course; the larger **Union Island**, a centre for sailors, and **Mustique**. On the latter there is only limited access for cruise ship passengers because the celebrities that stay here guard their privacy fiercely.

Grenada

The island that came off worst in Hurricane Ivan's merciless assault in September 2004, Grenada, just south of the Grenadines, did not waste any time in getting back on her feet. Only two months after the mighty hurricane had swept across the 35 by 20km (21- by 12-mile) island, killing 39 people and causing damage and destruction to 90 percent of the island, two cruise ships were greeted by bands, bunting and bravado. Already new shoots were emerging in the torn down forests covering the mountainous interior, and with a massive effort from the population, many of whom had lost their homes, and finan-

Bequia is best

Although good diving is available off St Vincent, if you are going to Bequia, save the experience until then. With more than 30 dive sites, Bequia is renowned for its underwater scenery.

cial aid from the other Caribbean islands and the rest of the international community, clearing up and rebuilding was well underway.

Known as the Spice Island, Grenada is not only the world's second largest exporter of nutmeg but also grows more spices per square kilometre than anywhere else on the planet. This will be evident by the line of hard-selling spice vendors waiting to welcome you ashore at **St George's**, the island capital. However, nutmeg trees were severely damaged by Hurricane Ivan and production on Grenada declined by about 75 per cent. Cocoa has since replaced it as the island's main crop.

Sailors down the centuries have rated St George's one of the world's prettiest harbours. Horseshoe-shaped and set in a long-dormant volcanic crater, it is a natural harbour flanked by two forts (Fort George and Fort Frederick) and has colourful French colonial-style buildings ranged along the waterfront.

Ferries and schooners can dock alongside the harbour, while cruise ships dock at **Melville Street Pier**, the other side of the promontory on which sits Fort George, where there is a visitors' welcome centre (with telephones, maps, shops and information). Just across the road and up a block is the city's market, where you can find spices, cocoa, hot sauces, jams and jellies as well as fresh produce. This area is known as Baytown and is joined to the Carenage by a tunnel for vehicles.

From the Spice Island, the fruit of the nutmeg tree

Pedestrians walk over the hill along Halifax Street and Young Street.

The Carenage

The harbour and promenade is known as the **Carenage**, where you find old warehouses, small shops and offices, and a selection of bars and restaurants. Many of these are on the first floor above shops, allowing the sea breezes to blow through wide open windows with a glorious view of the harbour. You will see plenty of seafood – including conch – on the menus and some traditional Grenadian dishes, made with *tatu* (armadillo), *manicou* (opossum) and iguana, from the island's forests, although these are less common now.

The Carenage

The cafés like the rest of St George's are very enjoyable. So is a visit to the ice cream parlour on the harbour front which has a delicious range of spice-based flavours.

On Young Street, off the Carenage near the cafés, there is the small **Grenada National Museum** (Mon–Fri 9am–4.30pm, Sat 10.30am–1pm; charge), where exhibits include a bathtub used by Empress Joséphine Bonaparte; and Market Square, which has a lively Saturday market. The second right from Young into Church Street, leads you to the site of St Andrew's Church and the Cathedral, constructed in 1830 and destroyed by the hurricane in 2004.

Southern Caribbean

St Vincent & The Grenadines, **Grenada**, **Trinidad & Tobago**, **Aruba & Curaçao (Lesser Antilles)**

Location: St Vincent & The Grenadines (capital Kingstown) lie 160km (100 miles) to the west of Barbados and just north of **Grenada** (St George's), the most southerly of the Windward Islands, toward the bottom of the Lesser Antilles chain. Grenada has two small dependent territories: Carriacou and Petit Martinique. The most southerly Caribbean island, **Trinidad** (Port of Spain), lies 20km (12 miles) off the coast of Venezuela. Together with **Tobago**, 34km (21 miles) to the northeast, Trinidad forms an independent nation within the British Commonwealth. **Aruba** (Oranjestad) and **Curaçao** (Willemstad) are the most westerly of the Lesser Antilles and with Bonaire (not a port of call) form the ABC Islands. Aruba and Curaçao are constituent countries of the Kingdom of the Netherlands, together with Sint Maarten and the Netherlands. Bonaire, Saba and Sint Eustatius are special municipalities within the Netherlands.

Time zones: UTC/GMT -4 (all the islands)

Population: 105,000 (St Vincent & The Grenadines); 108,000 (Grenada); 1,228,000 (Trinidad & Tobago); 106,000 (Aruba); 142,000 (Curaçao). Language: English/patois (St Vincent & The Grenadines, Grenada, Trinidad & Tobago); Dutch/Papiamento (Aruba, Curaçao).

Money matters: St Vincent & The Grenadines and Grenada: the East Caribbean dollar (EC$); Trinidad and Tobago: Trinidad and Tobago dollar (TT$); Aruba: Aruban florin/guilder (Af/AWG); Curaçao: the Netherlands Antilles florin (NAf) also known as the Netherlands Antilles guilder (ANG). The islands all accept US dollars (US$).

Telephone & Internet: The dialling code is +784 (St Vincent & The Grenadines); +473 (Grenada); +868 (Trinidad & Tobago); +297 (Aruba); +59 99 (Curaçao). The internet is widely available.

Calendar highlights: Carnival: Trinidad (Feb/Mar), Grenada (Aug), Curaçao (Jan); Bequia: Bequia Regatta (Easter); Grenadines: Mustique Blues Festival (Jan–Feb); Trinidad: 3-day Hosay Islamic Festival (April).

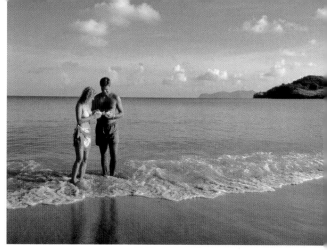

Couple enjoying the beach in Grenada

Grand Anse Beach

Just a water-taxi ride around the bay to the south of the harbour is **Grand Anse**, one of the finest 3km (2-mile) stretches of white sand in the Caribbean. The short, breezy journey by water-taxi, which depart regularly from the cruise ship terminal, is much more fun than going by land.

There are strict rules about any kind of development on Grenada, which applies particularly to beaches. Effectively, this comes down to nothing taller than a palm tree and nothing close to the water's edge being allowed. A selection of watersports is available here.

Dramatic Sights

A drive through the interior takes in some dramatic sights – waterfalls, mountain valleys, rainforests, lakes and volcanic craters. Although the island is small, driving can be slow, hot and tiring on roads that are sometimes barely adequate, so don't be too ambitious when you have limited time. You can rent a car from agencies along the Carenage but you may prefer to take an organised tour or hire a taxi for a guided tour (negotiate the price before setting off). Local buses are slow and overcrowded but can be an interesting experience.

Most of the dive sites – coral reefs and shipwrecks – are within easy reach of the shore. Snorkellers can reach them from the beach or, occasionally, by a short boat trip. However, the dive site considered the best – **Kick 'em Jenny**, a large submerged volcano – is further offshore.

Deep-sea fishing is big in Grenada and trips can be organised through charter companies in the harbour to catch marlin, kingfish and yellowfin tuna. The Spice Island Game Fishing Tournament, at the end of January, is a major event in the island's sporting calendar.

Swim amongst waterfalls

National Parks

The **Grand Etang National Park and Forest Reserve** is a rainforest covering the mountainous backbone of the island, with a volcanic crater-turned-lake at its centre. There are hiking and nature trails, and fishing and boating in the shadow of **Mount Qua Qua**, a 700-metre (2,300ft) peak. On the way back, it's worth making a detour to the 15-metre (50ft) **Annandale Falls**.

At the **Gouyave Nutmeg Processing Cooperative** (Mon–Fri 8am–4pm; charge), north of the capital, you can see how the island's most famous export is handled. The **Dougaldston Spice Estate** is a working spice plantation,

growing and processing spices. Here you can buy nutmeg, cinnamon, cloves and other spices.

Belmont Estate (tel: 473-442 9524, www.belmontestate. net) is a working plantation offering tours of the organic farm, gardens, heritage museum and cocoa processing facilities. Formerly a nutmeg plantation, cocoa has since replaced it as the island's main crop. The organic cocoa produced here (and by other local organic farmers) is used to make the exquisite chocolate produced by the **Grenada Chocolate Factory** (www.grenadachocolate.com). If you buy some, don't be worried about it melting in the heat of the tropics. It is so pure that it doesn't melt, but if concerned, buy their cocoa powder instead.

Along the same road, on the east coast, is the **River Antoine Rum Distillery** (Mon– Sat 9am–4pm; free tours), where rum is still made using 18th-century methods.

In the northeast at the tip of the island, **Levera National Park** stretches inland from coral-reef protected white sandy beaches to a lake and mangrove swamp full of exotic plants and birdlife.

Trinidad and Tobago

The southernmost islands in the Caribbean archipelago, Trinidad and Tobago are not like the other islands to the north, as they are really small chunks of Venezuela that have

Trinidad, city of Carnival

drifted away from the mainland. As a result, their geography, flora and fauna are more of a South American nature and has plenty of natural attractions. Tobago is still very different from Trinidad – it is much smaller, less developed and more laid-back and tranquil.

Trinidad

Cruise ships dock at the modern complex in one of the English-speaking Caribbean's most vibrant cities. Fast-paced **Port of Spain** is unique for its ethnic diversity and cultural richness, and mixes styles with a Latin flair arising from its proximity to Venezuela only 11km (7 miles) away. Elegant French-Creole townhouses with distinctive gingerbread fretwork and ornate wrought-iron balconies nestle beneath modern, smoked-glass corporate blocks.

This is where the carnival of all Caribbean carnivals climaxes on the streets over the two days before Ash Wednesday, exploding with the colours of thousands of masqueraders driven by turbo-charged soca music, calypso and melodic steel pan.

A Tour of the Capital

Port of Spain and its suburbs sprawl across a plain that slopes gently from the foothills of the Northern Range down to the Gulf of Paria. On the waterfront, there are plenty of craft shops to peruse as you leave the ship. To the left, on Wrightson Road, is the Breakfast Shed, known for cheap, authentic Creole and East Indian cuisine: fresh fish, fried, stewed or served in a peppery-hot broth laced with ground provisions such as dasheen, eddoes, cassava or green figs (small green bananas) and heavy with dumplings.

Across from the terminal, the Brian Lara Promenade (named after the record-breaking Trinidadian cricketer) in **Independence Square**, is flanked by modern buildings. Here people gather to play chess or enjoy the free soca, steelpan, jazz or

Carnival in Trinidad

Trinidad Carnival has earned its reputation as one of the greatest shows on earth and is the culmination of a year's worth of preparation. During the weekend before the start of Lent, a Carnival King, Queen and Calypso Monarch are crowned to great fanfare. Then from 4am on Carnival Monday until midnight on the Tuesday, normal life in the capital dissolves into one wild and euphoric party that anyone can join. Starting with J'ouvert (opening of day), revellers emerge covered in mud (or paint) portraying demons and banging tins and drums. Later the mas' bands – groups of up to 10,000 people in themed elaborate costumes – parade past the judging stands throughout the city, accompanied by ear-splitting soca, until the street party ends at Las' Lap. Then on Ash Wednesday the preparations for next year begin…

Steel pans, or drums

gospel concerts. Vendors sell coconuts and doubles – an inexpensive East Indian snack of curried chick peas in batter, garnished with mango or coconut chutney and fiery pepper sauce. Further east on South Quay, a museum in the old Spanish **Fort San Andres** (Tue–Fri 9am–5pm) tells the story of Port of Spain and hosts exhibitions by young local artists. The wooden terracotta-painted fort was once Port of Spain's main defence against the British troops.

Although most cruise lines offer guided taxi tours of the city and half- or whole-day excursions outside, it is more exciting (and safe) to walk around the city centre for a couple of hours during the day. For travelling out of the city, there are fixed-rate taxis at the rank opposite Frederick Street on Independence Square and cheaper shared-route taxis at Woodford Square.

British-built **Fort George** is just a short taxi or bus ride into the hills above the western suburb of St James, and offers both a breathtaking panorama of the city and views of the islands off the Chaguaramas Peninsula.

Queen's Park Savannah

Frederick Street is the city's main artery, leading north to **Queen's Park Savannah,** via Woodford Square where you will find the imposing **Red House** parliament building. At the top of Frederick Street, opposite Memorial Park is the **National Museum and Art Gallery** (Tue–Sat 10am–6pm, Sun 2–6pm). The Savannah plays an integral part in Trinidadian life and is the major venue for carnival competitions and cultural shows. On the western flank of the Savannah are the **Magnificent Seven**, a row of early 20th-century colonial mansions, which are superb examples of idiosyncratic Trini-Creole architecture. To the north are the **Emperor Valley Zoo** (daily 9.30am–6pm; charge), the pretty **Botanic Gardens** (daily 6am–6.30pm) and the **President's House**.

> ### Steel drums
>
> Steel pan music originated in Trinidad in the 1930s when it was discovered that discarded oil drums produced a wonderful sound when beaten with a stick or the hand.

A Taste of the Island

A choice of half- and whole-day excursions are available outside Port of Spain. West of town is the **Blue Basin Waterfall**, north of Diego Martin; **Maqueripe beach** at the end of the beautiful Tucker Valley; and the **Gasparee Caves** on Gaspar Grande island, a 20-minute round-trip boat ride from the Crews Inn Marina (call 634 4364 to book tours). **Maracas Bay**, Trinidad's most popular beach, is a 40-minute drive north of the capital, while to the east is the **Maracas Waterfall**, just up the valley from the original Spanish capital, St Joseph.

Other destinations include **El Tucuche**, the second highest peak (a day's strenuous hike); **Mount St Benedict** monastery, with panoramic views of the central plain; and the **Asa Wright Nature Centre**, internationally known for birdwatching. Trinidad has a magnificent variety of bird species. Southeast of the capital is the **Caroni Bird Sanctuary**, where the national bird, the Scarlet Ibis, roosts at dusk.

Tobago's Capital

While Port of Spain is very much a city, **Scarborough**, the capital of Trinidad's sister isle, **Tobago**, has both the look and feel of a small provincial town, and most of it can be explored on foot (with a few steep inclines) in a morning. After the multi-cultural mix of Trinidad, Tobago's predominantly Afro-Creole culture and lifestyle is noticeable, as is the slower pace.

Cruise ship passengers disembark at the modern terminal opposite the busy market, a good spot for sampling hearty Tobagonian cooking, such as curried crab and dumplings. The terminal has basic amenities, and taxis can be hired outside.

In town, the main attractions are the **Botanic Gardens**, the **House of Assembly** on James Park and the **Fort King George** complex, which houses the excellent **Tobago Museum** (Mon–Fri 9am–5pm; charge) and has fantastic views over the town and up the coast.

As the island is only 40km (26 miles) long and 15km (9 miles) wide, it is possible to reach virtually anywhere within a couple of hours by car – idyllic white sand beaches and coral reefs teeming with marine life; superb scuba diving, snorkelling and water sports; waterfalls, volcanic hills and the Western Hemisphere's oldest protected rainforest; abundant bird and wildlife; and authentic Afro-Creole culture. The latter can be found at its vibrant best in the inland hilltop villages of **Les Coteaux**, **Whim** and **Moriah**, major venues for July's Heritage Festival in which Tobago explores its cultural past with lively music and processions.

Goat race

Buccoo is the venue for the traditional goat races that bring Tobago's Easter festivities to a close. Goats are trained, for months in advance, to run the 100 metres (328ft) to the finish line with a handler holding on to them by a rope.

Beautiful Beaches and Reefs

Close to Scarborough is the developed southwest end of the island, where most tourist activity is centred round the luxury resorts and hotels at **Crown Point** and

Store Bay. Glass-bottomed boats can be hired at Store Bay for trips out to **Buccoo Reef** and the Nylon Pool, while the beach at **Pigeon Point** has become a familiar Caribbean icon.

Inland from the windward (southern) coast the **Hillsborough Reservoir** is a favourite birdwatching spot. Further down the coast, the **Argyll Waterfall**, best in the rainy season, is a 10-minute walk from the road. Nearby, you can tour the **Tobago Cocoa Estate** (tours Mon–Fri 9am and 11am, charge), learn about cocoa growing, the chocolate-making process, buy their single-estate fine chocolate and try other local culinary delights.

Fort King George

Divers and nature lovers head for **Speyside** and **Charlotteville**, at the eastern tip. These two fishing villages are spectacularly positioned at the foot of forested hills and are the jumping-off points for some of the best diving in the region.

The beaches to head for (both for bathing and for turtle watching) are on the northern coast: Turtle Beach (Great Courland Bay), Castara, Englishman's Bay, Parlatuvier, Bloody Bay and Man-o-War Bay are all superb.

Aruba and Curaçao

Just off the coast of Venezuela in the 'deep Caribbean' lie the small islands of Aruba and Curaçao which have a Dutch

Crossing a baby natural bridge, Aruba

heritage. Aruba has been self-governing since 1986, but since 2010, when the Netherlands Antilles was dissolved, both islands are now constituent countries of the Kingdom of the Netherlands.

Inland the terrain is hilly, providing a very different kind of flora and fauna from the rest of the Caribbean.

Aruba's Capital

Excellent beaches, world-class shopping, giant casinos, stunning sea views and wild tracts of desert landscape scattered with giant boulders and exotic cacti are all within reach of **Oranjestad**, Aruba's capital – teeming with people, especially when several ships have docked at the three **Aruba Port Authority terminals**.

Within a few minutes' walk, to the right, you will find the shop-lined L.G. Smith Boulevard, home to **Seaport Market**, and the equally extensive, **Royal Plaza**, crammed with smart shops. Straight ahead is the capital's main shopping area, **Caya G.F. Betico Croes**, where pretty Dutch- and Spanish-style buildings house stores selling cameras, jewellery and alcohol. You can also pick up Delft china, Dutch cheese, Danish silverware and embroidery from Madeira paying low levels of duty and without any sales tax.

For local colour, head to **Paardenbaai** (Schooner Harbour), which is crammed with brightly painted little boats and craft stalls selling the boat-owners' wares. A few streets up in Wilheminastraad are some magnificent examples of 16th- and 17th-century Dutch architecture. Back on the waterfront is **Wilhemina Park**, a lovely tropical garden.

A Bet on the Beach

Some of the world's best beaches can be found on Aruba. On the island's northwest coast are **Eagle Beach** and **Palm Beach**, long stretches of snowy-white sand bordered by casinos and hotels, which will (for a fee) provide all the facilities you need to swim, sunbathe and lunch in style, although use of the beaches is free. The aptly named **Baby Beach** at the southeastern end of the island has shallow waters and soft sand that is perfect for young children.

En route lies Aruba's oldest village, **San Nicolas**, a former oil refinery and port which is now full of unusual shops and alfresco cafés. Nearer the port, **Spaan Lagoen** (Spanish Lagoon) is a scenic spot which was once the haunt of pirates.

Aruba's sights

With plenty of taxis at the terminal and good tourist information available, it's easy to explore Aruba independently, but for discovering the delights of the **Barcadera Reef** and for sailing trips and jeep safaris, it's best to opt for a cruise line excursion.

The dramatic, rocky land-

Diverse dishes

For lunch, you are spoilt for choice with Aruba's diverse population – of Portuguese, Spanish, Venezuelan, Indian, Pakistani, African and Dutch descent – offering a wide range of dishes.

Willemstad

scape of the north includes the famous **Natural Bridge**, hewn by nature from limestone albeit now collapsed (a baby bridge is also here however). Fantastical, rare boulder formations, some with Amerindian drawings on them can be seen at **Ayo** and **Casibari**, and from the 168-metre (551ft) **Hooiberg**, you have a fine view of the fields of gigantic cacti in **Arikok National Park**. Bizarre rock formations can also be seen in the cave systems of **Fontein** and **Guadirikiri**.

A Tropical Amsterdam

Curaçao, 60km long by 11 km (38 by 7 miles) wide, is the largest island in the Dutch Antilles and home to more than 50 different nationalities, who give the place a liberal, cosmopolitan and welcoming atmosphere.

Amsterdam's influence is evident in the architecture of the

 capital, **Willemstad**. The mega cruise ships dock at the

port's US$9-million terminal, a short walk from town, but smaller ships have the privilege of sailing up St Ana Bay, past the swing-aside **Queen Emma Bridge**, to the older terminal on the Otrobanda (western) side of town.

First colonised by the Dutch in the 1630s, Willemstad is resplendent with fine examples of 17th- 18th- and 19th-century Dutch and Spanish colonial architecture, the best of which are along the bay front.

Walking across the wobbly Queen Emma Bridge (or hop on the free ferry) to the Punda (eastern) side of town you will find the colourful **Floating Market**, lined with boats from Colombia and Venezuela. As you come off the bridge, **Fort Amsterdam** is on the right, a sandstone fortress on the waterfront, which dates from 1700 and now houses the Governor's Palace. A mid-18th century church stands nearby. At one corner of the fort and leading from the bridge is **Breederstraat**, one of Willemstad's best shopping streets and gateway to the main commercial district.

Venezuelan Ports of Call

Isla Margarita, just 40km (25 miles) off Venezuela's coast, and **La Guaira**, the main port for Caracas, 10km (6 miles) away, feature on many itineraries leaving from Puerto Rico. Margarita, once famous for its pearls, is really two islands connected by an 18km (11-mile) sandbar of broken shells. By this sandbank is the Laguna de la Restinga where you can take a boat trip through the mangroves. The western peninsula (Macanao) is fairly barren and undeveloped but has some good beaches. The main sights are in the eastern part, with duty-free shopping, a market, casinos and colonial architecture in Porlamar.

From La Guaira you can visit Caracas, Venezuela's cosmopolitan capital, or view it from the top of Monte Avila. Nearby Colonia Tovar is a beautiful 19th-century town in the mountains with a good museum.

A Cultural Experience

The **Maritime Museum** (Mon–Sat 9am–5pm; charge), on van den Brandhofstraat 7, Scharloo Abou, near the floating market, has some fascinating exhibits. The museum arranges harbour tours by water taxi. Also within walking distance of the Queen Emma Bridge (on Van Leeuwenhoekstraat in Otrobanda) is the **Curaçao Museum** (Mon–Fri 8.30am–4.30pm, Sun 10am–4pm; charge), a 19th-century military hospital building that holds colonial antiques and artefacts of the region's Caiquetio tribes. The **Kurá Holanda Museum** (Klipstraat 9; Tue–Sat 10am–5pm; charge), on the site of a former slave yard is an anthropological museum and focuses on the African slave trade and Antillean art. Northeast of town is the **Senior Curaçao Liqueur Factory** (Mon–Fri 8am–noon, 1–5pm), where you can discover the secret of the original liqueur's invention and have a taste too.

Within an hour's drive is the **Christoffel National Park** (Mon–Sat 8am–4pm; charge), a large nature reserve in the far north of the island, with rare orchids and cacti. Its underwater equivalent is the **Curaçao Seaquarium** (daily 8am–5pm; charge), which has more than 350 species of sea life.

You can see orchids in Christoffel National Park

The **Hato Caves** are a network of subterranean limestone caverns, north of the capital. The caves have a mirror-like underground lake and stunning rock formations. At **San Jofat**, where members of the Dutch royal family have holiday homes, you can join a boat to go snorkelling, and see some of Curaçao's bays and inlets.

Cruising and the Environment

With gargantuan vessels carrying up to and over 3,000 passengers dock-ing at tiny island ports, cruising can't fail to make an impact on the en-vironment. However, cruise lines are becoming more aware of how their industry affects the Caribbean region and there is growing recognition that land and sea must work together. Still, there is much work to do and the critics say:

• The logistics of providing first-class modern services and efficient ex-cursions is an enormous challenge for small and under-resourced islands. Many still require massive investment.

• Restaurants and hotels don't benefit, as everything is provided and al-ready paid for on the ships. Many passengers don't even disembark.

• Passengers don't tend to spend much on the islands except on duty-free goods, usually from internationally owned outlets.

• Ships don't buy enough local produce, stocking up before they go.

• Ships generate a large amount of waste that pollutes the sea.

The cruise lines claim:

• Their industry provides jobs, not just on the islands (where some 60,000 jobs are created) but also on the ships and local tour operators and taxi companies benefit.

• Cruises provide a 'taster' to many who return as land-based tourists.

• Modern ships now have built-in waste management systems and re-cycling centres, conforming to international law, which bans dumping food waste and sewage in coastal waters and plastics anywhere.

How you can help:

• Disembark at every port.

• Check out tours at the quayside, or sign up for locally run tours.

• Use local restaurants and cafés.

• Buy island-made souvenirs and visit museums and churches.

• Only take photos of people with their permission and offer a tip.

Although cruise lines are powerful, now a more conciliatory atmosphere prevails. A proper partnership benefits everyone, including the traveller.

A–Z TRAVEL TIPS

A Summary of Practical Information

A Activities 183
B Booking a Cruise . 177
C Choosing a Cabin . 174
  Choosing a Cruise 171
  Climate 181
  Counting the Cost 178
  Cruise Line
    Information 187
  Cruising with
    Children 174
D Dining on Board . . 185
  Disabled
    Travellers 175
E Etiquette 184
F Food and Drink . . . 184
G Gay and Lesbian
    Cruises 172
  Getting There 172
H Health 179
  Home Ports 175
I Internet 184

L Life on Board 182
  Life on Shore 187
M Money 185
  Medical Care 185
P Passports and
    Visas 180
  Preparing for the
    Trip 177
R Religious Services . 183
S Ship Facilities 185
  Shore Excursions . 187
T Theme Cruises . . . 172
  Telephone 183
  Tipping 179
  Tourist Information 189
  Tours 187
  Travel Agents 177
  Travel Insurance . . 179
W Weddings 176
  What to Bring 182
  What to Wear 182

CHOOSING A CRUISE

The first decision to make when choosing a cruise is how long do you want – or can afford – to go for. Then you must consider what type would suit you best – a theme cruise, one packed with entertainment, a romantic sailing ship, or lots of ports of call. Most people find that a 10-day cruise is ideal: one week for exploring both on- and offshore, with three days at sea.

TYPES OF CRUISE

Do your research. Each cruise line offers a different experience: the mega ships of Carnival Cruises, Princess Cruises and Royal Caribbean provide the whole big-ship experience – Broadway-style shows, different dining options, lots of deck sports and a high proportion of balcony cabins. Many also lease or own private islands or beaches where you can enjoy a barbecue and watersports. In contrast, a small or mid-sized ship, such as those belonging to Oceania Cruises, the smaller Holland America Line ships, or the upscale vessels of Seabourn or Silversea, will be more restful.

There are small, luxurious ships that call at the harbours favoured by the yachting set – Virgin Gorda, St-Barths and St-Martin's Marigot Bay. Mid-sized ships, on which the emphasis is on the destinations as much as what's on board, may roam the Southern Caribbean, skimming the coast of South America or venturing down to the Amazon.

Star Clippers, Sea Cloud, and Windstar Cruises are the ones to choose for the romance of a sailing ship, whether it's a square rigger or floating gin palace. *(See page 187 for contact details.)*

European-operated lines, such as Costa Cruises, tend to have a more international flavour, while P&O and Fred Olsen carry mainly British travellers, and US-run vessels have a predominantly American passenger list.

Know your cruise lines and ships. Although cruise lines may sound similar in their advertisements, they offer different holiday experiences at different rates. Some specialise in great food, while others have a vast array shipboard amenities, such as rock-climbing walls.

Once you've decided on a particular cruise line, remember that not all ships in a fleet are the same. Newer ones tend to be more expensive, but come with the latest features and more cabins with balconies. Apart from the cruise line's website, a top source of information is the annual *Berlitz Complete Guide to Cruising and Cruise Ships*, which provides exhaustive reviews of more than 250 vessels.

Getting there. Once you've chosen your cruise, talk to a travel agent, tourist board or airline company to determine the best way to get to the embarkation point. You may wish to stay longer by buying an 'open jaw' return and flying, say, into Miami and out of Barbados.

THEME CRUISES

There is a wide range of specially designed theme cruises that cater for a huge range of interests, lifestyles, hobbies and niche markets. You name it and there's probably a cruise for it, from vampires and Goths' conventions to hard-core boot camp fitness voyages.

Theme cruises are usually arranged by cruise organisers – individuals, small companies, special interest groups, and non-profit organisations working hand-in-hand with the cruise companies – not the cruise line itself. In this sense, the ships are 'hired out' by the cruise lines to the specific groups. Affinity groups are also a natural market for niche cruises.

African-American cruises. A growing segment of the affinity market are cruises catering for African-American travellers. Blue World Travel (tel: 800-466 2719; www.festivalatsea.com), has earned a stellar reputation for its Festival at Sea cruises. The cruises (usually on Carnival ships), run several times a year and feature lectures on African-American culture, Motown music nights and African-attire dinner parties.

Gay and Lesbian cruises. There's a thriving market for gay and lesbian cruise charters. Big organisers like Atlantis Events (tel: 310-859 8800; www.atlantisevents.com) and RSVP Vacations (tel: 1-

800-328 7787; www.rsvpvacations.com) can fill the world's biggest ships for exclusive gay and lesbian charters, featuring big-name gay entertainers and guest speakers, as well as a huge range of parties and excursions. Cruising is generally very gay friendly. Along with fostering a comfortable shipboard environment, these ships also stop at islands known to be welcoming to gay people.

Culinary cruises. Focusing on food and wine, these cruises range from those that offer cookery demonstrations by masterchefs to others that concentrate on a regional cuisine such as Taste of the Islands cruises, which highlight French West Indian or Latin Caribbean cooking. There is also a growing trend for ships to have high-tech cookery studios on board and cookery classes under the guidance of expert guest chefs.

Educational cruises. Part of the growing trend for combining education with travel, an organisation called University at Sea (tel: 800-422 0711 in the US; www.universityatsea.com) runs an innovative series of fully accredited, continuing education courses. Many of these cruises are tax-deductible in the US.

Health cruises. There are speciality cruises devoted to yoga, body-building, martial arts, meditation, stress reduction, aerobics, massage, tai chi and weight loss – including Cruise To Lose voyages on Carnival's ships, or Cruise to Run (tel: 1-877-562 8669; www.cruisetorun.com), with organised fun runs in every port.

Musical cruises. Music is another major subject for theme cruises, with choices that range from jazz, classical, opera, soul, salsa, gospel, country and western, dixieland, 1950s' retro rock 'n' roll, and big band orchestras.

Naturist cruises are offered by several organisations, usually on smaller, privately-chartered ships. One of the more established is Bare Necessities Tours (tel: 1-800-743 0405; www.bare-necessities.com).

Sporty cruises. Sport is another popular theme, with golf being one of the favourites. Fred Olsen Cruises and Silversea Cruises are renowned for their onboard golf programmes, complete with resident pro and organised rounds at the world's top courses, while other golf themes are offered by specialist tour operators, such as Golf Ahoy (tel: 780-415 5442; www.golfahoy.com), which will team up enthusiasts on board and arrange everything in port for a seamless golf vacation (wisely including spa treatments for non-golfing partners).

CHOOSING A CABIN

First of all, envisage how you will be spending your time during the cruise. If you love sightseeing, you may not need an expensive cabin as you won't be spending much time in it. But if you think you're going to spend sea days eating, reading and napping in the privacy of your cabin or relaxing on your balcony, then you would be advised to go for the more expensive option – a large cabin.

Sailboats, and even small cruising yachts, lean toward tiny, serviceable staterooms. Older, larger ships also tend to have small cabins without balconies that encourage guests to get out and about on the ship. Usually, the newer the ship the more spacious the cabin, and you will always have a private bathroom.

The choice will be between an inside cabin, outside cabin, balcony cabin or suite. Specific cabins can be pre-booked on all ships, although some cruise lines charge for this facility. On large ships, the least expensive cabins tend to be windowless, interior ones.

CRUISING WITH CHILDREN

Teen discos, children-only swimming pools, 'Circus at Sea' lessons and supervised, age-related activity programmes have become an intrinsic part of modern megaship cruising. Carnival and Royal Caribbean have indoor and outdoor children's facilities on their biggest ships, with huge areas dedicated to children.

The facilities on *Disney Wonder*, *Disney Dream* and *Disney Magic* are superb (with special adult-only areas for those who need a break from children), while Princess, Royal Caribbean and Norwegian Cruise Line all have good children's facilities and entertainment. Among the British cruise lines, P&O is excellent and Cunard's *Queen Mary 2* has the largest nursery at sea, staffed by highly qualified nannies. P&O and Princess ships offer a night nursery, providing free care for sleeping infants while the parents relax.

HOME PORTS

Most of the big ships are based at Florida's three main ports: Miami (Royal Caribbean, Carnival, Celebrity and Norwegian Cruise Line), Fort Lauderdale/Port Everglades (Holland America, Princess, Celebrity and Royal Caribbean) and Port Canaveral (Disney Cruise Line and some Carnival, Royal Caribbean and Holland America ships).

US travellers who choose not to fly can sail to the Caribbean and the Yucatán directly from ports such as Jacksonville, Tampa, Galveston and New Orleans, often within driving distance of home. There are home ports on Caribbean islands with international airports. San Juan, Puerto Rico, and Bridgetown in Barbados are two of the busiest regional home ports.

British-run lines, like P&O Cruises and Fred Olsen Cruises have cut back on their Caribbean fly-cruise programmes and base many ships year-round in Britain, only offering three-week Atlantic crossings and cruises in the Caribbean.

DISABLED TRAVELLERS

Cruising can be an ideal holiday for travellers with disabilities. Wheelchair users will find that most ships provide a relaxing, sociable setting while visiting lots of destinations. Take the advice of a specialist cruise travel agent before booking; make sure they provide specific information about airport transfers, boarding the ship, the facilities on board and the cabin itself.

All new ships have cabins adapted to wheelchair users, although in varying degrees. If you're uncomfortable walking long distances, consult the deck plans online, and avoid the very biggest ships, getting around with a stick or walking frame can be exhausting.

Another tip when planning a cruise is to choose a voyage with as few tender ports (those where the ship anchors outside the port and guests are ferried ashore) as possible. It is much easier for the less able to get ashore down a gangway than by climbing onto a lifeboat that is bobbing up and down.

Some of the best options are escorted Caribbean cruise packages for wheelchair users, organised in the US by Accessible Journeys (tel: 610-521 0339; www.disabilitytravel.com), or for UK cruisers, to take specialist cruise holiday advice from Accessible Travel (tel: 01452-729 739; www.accessibletravel.co.uk).

Older cruise ships do not generally provide special facilities for those with hearing difficulties, although Crystal's two ships, the *Queen Mary 2* and some of the Celebrity fleet have special headsets in their cinemas. Newer ships have some signage in braille – on lift buttons and cabin door numbers.

WEDDINGS

Cruise lines compete with one another to offer wedding, honeymoon and renewal of vows packages, always at a price. The bigger lines have in-house wedding coordinators who will arrange everything from the flowers to the cake. Princess Cruises can hold weddings officiated by the captain, as can Celebrity Cruises, P&O Cruises and Azamara Club Cruises. On other lines, you can bring your own celebrant on board but must hold the ceremony while the ship is in port.

Many ships have wedding chapels, although these tend not to be very exciting. Ask if you can have the ceremony on the bridge or find a prettier spot on deck. Disney Cruise Line will allow couples to hold wedding ceremonies on the beach at Castaway Cay, its private island (although the official exchange of vows and paperwork must be held ashore, before the ship sails), while Holland America Line can arrange weddings at Half Moon Cay, its own private beach.

An alternative is to hold the nuptials in a romantic location on dry land in one of the ports of call and have either a reception, or a honeymoon, or both, at sea, organised by the cruise line. There are endless options for getting married ashore if you arrange it independently, but several cruise lines offer special wedding packages, and Carnival and Princess will organise a shoreside wedding with a cruise, often using one of their private islands for the ceremony.

PREPARING FOR THE TRIP

Many cruise lines don't have in-house reservations agents but they will provide a toll-free number, send brochures and put you in touch with a local representative. You can find a specialist travel agent in your area through the UK's Association of Cruise Experts (ace) at www.cruiseexperts.org; the Cruise Lines International Association (clia) in the US, at www.cruising.org, or the International Cruise Council of Australasia (icca) at www.cruising.org.au.

BOOKING A CRUISE

Online

Travel websites, such as www.expedia.com, www.orbitz.com, and www.travelocity.com, all offer cruise bargains. Cruise-specific websites include www.choosingcruising.co.uk, www.cruisebrothers.com, www.cruise411.com, www.ecruise.co.uk, www.cruisecompete.com and www.cruiselocators.com.

Agents in the UK

- **The Cruise People,** 88 York Street, London W1H 1DP; tel: 020 7723 2450; www.cruisepeople.co.uk.
- **Cumbria Cruise Club,** Andrews Court, Andrews Way, Barrow-in-Furness, LA14 2UD; tel: 0800 540540; www.cumbriacruise.co.uk.
- **Ideal Cruising,** Admiral House, 193–199 London Road, Camberley, Surrey, GU15 3JT; tel: 0800 2315 520; www.idealcruising.co.uk.
- **Marion Owen Travel,** 23 Portland Street, Hull, HU2 8JX; tel: 01482 212525; www.marionowentravel.com.

- **Mundy Cruising,** Quadrant House, 80–82 Regent Street, London W1B 5JB; tel: 020 7734 4404; www.mundycruising.co.uk.

Agents in the US
- **Cruise.com** claims to be the largest website specialising in cruises on the internet, tel: 888-333 3116; www.cruise.com.
- **Cruise Holidays** has branches all over the US and Canada, tel: 866-336 1882; www.cruiseholidays.com.
- **Cruise Planners** has branches in Florida and California, tel: 1-888-387 7202; www.cruiseplannersforyou.com.
- **Cruise Store,** 55 Maple Street, East Longmeadow, MA 01028, tel: 800-732 2897; www.cruisestore.com.
- **Liberty Travel** has over 200 branches all along the East Coast, tel: 888-271 1584; www.libertytravel.com.

Agents in Australia and New Zealand:
- **Harvey World Travel,** tel: 1-300 855 492; www.harveyworld. com.au.
- **ecruising.travel;** Level 9, 64 Castlereagh Street, Sydney NSW 2000; tel: 1-300 369 848; www.ecruising.travel.
- **Worldwide Cruise Centre** (in Brisbane, Gold Coast, Melbourne and Sydney); tel: 1-300 897 590 (Brisbane), 1-300 137 445 (Gold Coast), 1-300 889 240 (Melbourne), 1-300 883 620 (Sydney); www.cruisecentre.com.au.
- **iCruise,** 101 Great South Road, Remuera, Auckland, NZ; tel: 0800 427 847; www.icruise.co.nz.

COUNTING THE COST

Generally, your booking price will cover your cabin and food in the main dining room – and there are plenty of extra costs.

Hidden extras. Items *included* in the price of the cruise: all food; all entertainment; use of the gym and sports facilities (but not always all of them); transfers from the port (usually); port taxes; room service (sometimes); shuttle buses into town (sometimes); flights (usually); use of the ship's self-service laundry (usually); use of the ship's library; the captain's cocktail party.

Items *not included*: alcoholic drinks (except on Silversea, Seabourn, SeaDream, Regent Seven Seas); tips (unless stated); travel insurance; spa treatments; shore excursions; medical care; internet access and telephone calls from the satellite phone. Some cruise lines also charge extra for the following: visits to the bridge; use of some sports equipment; 'premium' exercise classes such as yoga; mineral water in cabins; room service; tea and coffee and shuttle buses. Most charge extra for dining in the 'alternative' restaurants.

Tipping. On Silversea, Seabourn, SeaDream, Regent Seven Seas and Thomson, some or all of the tips are included in the price. Many lines, including Carnival, Disney and Royal Caribbean allow, or even insist for tips to be pre-paid, while others add a suggested amount automatically to your onboard account, or place an envelope for cash in the cabin on the final evening.

Regardless of tipping policy, ships carrying mainly Americans usually add a 15–18 percent gratuity to the bar bill 'for your convenience'. This is also common practice in the ships' spas. Passengers are expected to tip their waiter and cabin steward.

Travel insurance. You should always arrange comprehensive travel insurance to cover both yourself and your belongings. Shop around as rates vary. Make sure you are covered for emergency medical care, repatriation by air ambulance (essential for international travellers), accidental death, baggage and document loss, and trip cancellation.

HEALTH

Drinking water. In undeveloped areas away from resorts, it is best to avoid drinking tap water, especially after a hurricane when the water supply can be contaminated. In these areas, stick to bottled water, and avoid ice in your drinks.

Immunisation. No immunisations are required for travellers to the Caribbean, unless the traveller is coming from an infected or endemic area. However, it is a good idea to have a tetanus shot if you are not already covered. The main (though small) health risk to travellers on land in the Caribbean is infectious hepatitis or Hepatitis A. Although it is not a requirement, an injection of gamma globulin, administered as close as possible before departure, gives good protection against Hepatitis A. In addition, make sure you observe scrupulous personal hygiene, wash and peel fruit, and drink bottled water.

Insects. Mosquitoes are generally only a nuisance in port in the evening. To combat mosquitoes, pack a supply of insect repellent. Dengue-carrying mosquitoes bite during the day and present a small risk. The only area which usually carries a malaria risk is Hispaniola, more in Haiti than the Dominican Republic.

Sun protection. To the uninitiated 27–32°C (80–90°F) may sound 'just like summer temperatures back home'. Don't be fooled. The sun in the tropics is more direct than in temperate regions and is even stronger at sea as it reflects off the water. Bring a high-factor sunscreen and wear it whenever you go out.

AIDS presents a serious risk among all sectors of the population. In medical situations, the risk of being infected with hiv from an unsterilised needle is negligible, but if you prefer to bring your own, pack them in your baggage for the hold or they may be confiscated.

PASSPORTS AND VISAS

All passengers need a passport. It is common practice for passengers to hand over their passport at check-in until the end of the cruise, so make a photocopy to leave at home and another for the trip. Anyone wishing to visit a casino ashore may need to temporarily retrieve their passport from the purser.

Each passenger is given a cruise ship id card, which is swiped and checked every time you leave the ship; on modern ships, it doubles as a room key and a charge card. It also indicates whether any passengers are missing when the ship is about to depart.

Visas. Usually required for visitors from Eastern Europe and Cuba. All travellers must have, upon entering the islands, a return or onward ticket, and adequate funds to support themselves for the duration of their stay.

Cruise passengers arriving via a US gateway city such as Miami or Puerto Rico have to obtain Electronic System for Travel Authorisation (ESTA) before flying or sailing. This includes citizens from all of the 27 countries that previously participated in the US Visa Waiver Scheme. The ESTA requires that you have more than six months remaining on your passport before its expiry date and that you have a machine-readable passport to enter the United States. The fee for ESTA is US$14 per person. If unsure, check with the passport issuing authority in your home country that your passport is still valid.

WHEN TO GO

Climate. The Caribbean islands' proximity to the equator means that seasonal temperature changes are generally limited to less than 6°C (10°F). An added bonus is the trade winds, which bring regular, cooling breezes to most of the islands. Year round, temperatures average around 27°C (80°F) throughout the region. During the winter (Dec–Mar) night-time lows can drop to about 16°C (60°F), with daytime highs reaching as much as 32°C (90°F). Rainfall varies, ranging from around 50cm (20 inches) a year in Curaçao and up to 190cm (75 inches) a year in the Grenada rainforest.

Rainfall is generally heaviest during October and November, although June is wettest in Trinidad and Tobago. The 'dry' period coincides with the peak tourist season: December to April or May.

Hurricanes. One of the most damaging and dangerous phenomena affecting the Caribbean, hurricanes can strike from June to November and usually last from eight to 10 days. A hurricane warning is issued when the storm winds reach at least 119kph (74mph) and storm surges are expected in a specific area within 24 hours. Cruise ships are fitted with stabilisers (fins under the water level) to reduce the pitch and roll of the ship during bad weather.

WHAT TO BRING

Bring swimwear, walking shoes (for excursions), deck shoes, gym kit if you plan to work out, lots of sunblock, a brimmed sun hat, memory cards for your camera (expensive on board), binoculars, a small umbrella and light raincoat for sudden showers; seasickness remedies; and any regular medication you need.

What to wear. Cruising in the Caribbean can mean bringing two different wardrobes, one for the cruise and one for any overland travel afterwards. Some cruise lines, inspired by ncl's informal 'Freestyle' cruising, have done away with compulsory formal nights, although Cunard, Fred Olsen, Costa, P&O, Seabourn, Celebrity and Holland America Line are just a few that do have gala nights.

A week's cruise will generally have one or two formal nights and a mixture of casual and informal dress codes on the other nights:

Casual: Smart casual wear, but no shorts or vests.

Informal: Trousers and a smart shirt/jacket for men; cocktail dress for women.

Formal: Dinner jacket/tuxedo or dark suit for men; evening dress for women.

When away from beach or poolside, cover up – a simple T-shirt and a pair of shorts will do the trick. Nude or topless (for women) bathing is prohibited everywhere except for Guadeloupe, Martinique, St-Martin, St-Barthélemy and Bonaire. Guadeloupe, St-Martin, and Bonaire each have at least one designated nudist beach.

LIFE ON BOARD

Modern ships are as varied as resorts on land, catering for every age, taste and budget, with many of the new vessels each more innovative than the last.

ACTIVITIES AND ENTERTAINMENT

After dinner shows. The standard ship's evening entertainment, which could be stand-up comedy, a cabaret singer or a splashy Broadway-style show, includes two nightly performances, one after each dinner sitting.

Casinos. Gambling is a feature on most large ships and most casinos provide gaming lessons, as well as slot machines. Casinos in the Caribbean and on the ship tend to be more laid back than those in Las Vegas and elsewhere. Ships' casinos are closed when in port.

Las Vegas-style shows. Big 'production' shows can be spellbinding at sea, with some ships having technical facilities superior to those of a top theatre. Big-name musicals, futuristic circus shows and opera have all been staged on ships.

Live music. Ships nowadays offer everything from concert pianists to scantily clad female string quartets. Some have great tribute bands, talented jazz musicians and excellent orchestras.

Nightclubs and discos. With mixed age groups to cater for, the resident DJs generally play safe, including old favourites in their act.

Religious services. Interdenominational services are held on most cruise ships, conducted either by the captain or an on-board chaplain. Special Jewish charters will have a rabbi on board.

Talks and lectures. Many ships have guest lecturers and guest speakers who discuss topics related to the region or a specialist interest group.

COMMUNICATION

Telephones. Making telephone calls using a ship's satellite system is expensive, at up to US$12 per minute. It is cheaper to make calls from a land line in port, or from a mobile phone with a roaming agreement. All visitors with a roaming-enabled mobile phone will receive a signal in the Caribbean. Many ships now have their own network, when the vessel is at sea and out of range, but this is extremely expensive.

Public phonecards in several denominations are available from LIME (formerly Cable and Wireless) on those islands from which the company operates. Residents of the US and Canada can use AT&T USADirect public phones with a charge card, while some public phones allow European charge card holders to access their home operator.

Internet. All islands and most cruise terminals have internet cafes. All ships offer internet access although charges vary enormously. Many have WiFi for passengers with their own laptops, but a charge will be incurred.

ETIQUETTE

- Cruise lines are strict about the public areas being non-smoking, and some provide a cigar lounge for smokers.
- It is forbidden to film or record any of the ship's entertainers, for copyright reasons.
- If you are invited to dine with the captain, consider it an honour and reply immediately and observe the dress code *(see page 182)*.
- Visits to the bridge are rare for security reasons, although small ships operated by SeaDream and Star Clippers may allow access.

FOOD AND DRINK

That you can eat round the clock on a cruise is no exaggeration, so try to eat in moderation. Unless there is a 'speciality' restaurant on board, all the food on a cruise is included in the price.

Bars. Ships' bars range from the sophisticated to Irish theme pubs. All drinks bought in the bar can be signed for. Be aware that many ships will add an automatic 'gratuity' of 15–18 percent.

Cafés. Cappuccino and espresso from machines are usually better than cruise-ship tea and coffee. Afternoon tea is provided on many ships, with white-glove service, dainty cakes and sandwiches.

Drinking water. Although safe, the drinking water on cruise ships is heavily chlorinated and does not taste good to most people. All ships provide bottled water, although many charge for it.

Dining and restaurants. Some ships offer from two to four different dinner sittings in the dining room, while others have 'open seating', meaning you eat when you like and sit where you like. Smaller ships, carrying fewer than 100 passengers, tend to have just one sitting where all the passengers dine together.

As well as a main dining room, many ships have speciality restaurants where a small premium is charged for a different menu and more exclusive surroundings. Vegetarians, vegans and people with other dietary requirements are usually well catered for.

Room service. Usually included in the cost of the cruise, although some lower-budget cruise lines either charge for it or do not offer it. Many ships have tea- and coffee-making facilities in the cabins.

MONEY

Cruise operators encourage guests to register a credit card at the beginning of a voyage for on-board expenses. Otherwise, a bill will be compiled to be settled on the day of departure. While on board, whether a credit card is registered or not, everything is paid for using a special card issued by the ship.

Currency onboard most ships is the US dollar, although P&O, Fred Olsen and some Cunard vessels use sterling. There is usually an atm near the shops or casino, and exchange facilities at the customer relations desk, but rates are not competitive; use a local bank in port instead.

SHIP FACILITIES

Medical care. All cruise ships have a doctor and nurse on board (the exception being cargo ships or private yachts carrying fewer than 12 people). Facilities vary but a ship's doctor should be able to treat most ailments, including heart attacks and appendicitis. Seriously ill passengers may be stabilised until the ship arrives in port, or airlifted off. There is a fee for consulting the ship's doctor.

Norovirus (a common gastro-intestinal virus) occurs on cruise ships, as it does in hospitals and hotels, and it can spread quickly. If you have diarrhoea, vomiting and fever, report to the ship's doctor immediately. Avoid the virus by using the antiseptic hand wipes that are handed out on board and by washing hands scrupulously.

Cinema and TV. All ships offer in-cabin TV, usually showing satellite channels, movies and the ship's channels. Many ships have a cinema, too, showing first-run movies.

Gentlemen hosts. A 'gentleman host', also known as the dance host, is a feature on traditional cruises with Cunard, Crystal, Silversea, Holland America and Fred Olsen. Personable single men in their 50s and 60s are employed to act as dancing and dinner hosts to unaccompanied older women.

Library. The ship's library provides a quiet retreat and an endless source of free reading material, from novels to guidebooks.

The Purser. The Purser's Office (also called Reception, Guest Relations or the Information Desk) is the nerve centre of the ship for general passenger information and minor problems. This is the place to pick up dvds, ship-compiled newspapers and the ship's programme.

Spas. Sea spas now rival land-based health facilities in terms of the services they offer. You can treat yourself to facials and massages, have your teeth whitened, consult an acupuncturist or have a Botox treatment. All this comes at a price, however. Expect to pay over US$120 for a facial, a 55-minute massage, or a reflexology session. Book ahead for treatments on sea days as they are very popular.

Water sports. Some smaller ships, namely those of Star Clippers, SeaDream Yacht Club, Seabourn and Windstar have a water sports platform which can be lowered from the back of the ship. All of these carry their own equipment. The private islands of the big cruise lines usually have a beach with water sports facilities. Waterskiing, sailing, windsurfing, snorkelling and scuba diving are available on most islands and can be organised through hotels or with independent beach operators.

LIFE ON SHORE

Common politeness is as desirable on the islands as it is anywhere else. If you need to ask directions or advice always greet the person before asking a question. And a word of advice, slow down; life operates on a different timescale in the sleepy Caribbean.

SHORE EXCURSIONS

Although expensive, shore excursions do get snapped up quickly. You can often book them at the same time as buying your cruise, but take care not to book too many tours. A crowded schedule can be punishing on the pocket, as well as physically strenuous.

Assembly times can be as early as 5am and may entail 10 hours in a bus with little time at the sight. Practically all organised excursions will schedule in some shopping time.

Independent tours. You can see and do what you want if you are prepared to organise your own excursion, and it's often cheaper than a cruise-line tour. However, time is usually limited in port so you need to research the port of call first, bring a good map, and check that ferry and bus times coincide with the ship's arrival and departure. Remember, if you are late, the ship won't wait unless you are on a ship-organised tour, it is your responsibility to catch up at the next port.

CRUISE LINE INFORMATION

Azamara Club Cruises, US: 1050 Caribbean Way, Miami, FL 33132, tel: 877-999 9553; www.azamaraclubcruises.com. UK: tel: 0800 018 2525.

Carnival Cruise Lines, US: 3655 NW 87th Avenue, Miami, FL 33178, tel: 800-764 7419. UK: Carnival House, 5 Gainsford Street, London SE1 2NE, tel: 020 7940 4466; www.carnival.com.

Celebrity Cruises, US: 1050 Caribbean Way, Miami, FL 33132, tel: 800-647 2251; www.celebritycruises.com. UK: Building 3, Station Road, Addlestone, Weybridge, Surrey KT15 2PG, tel: 0844 493 2043; www.celebritycruises.co.uk.

Costa Cruises, US: 200 South Park Road, Suite 200, Hollywood, FL 33021, tel: 1-800-GO-COSTA. UK: 5 Gainsford Street, London SE1 2NE, tel: 0845 351 0552; www.costacruises.co.uk.

Crystal Cruises, US: Crystal Cruises, 2049 Century Park East, Suite 1400, Los Angeles, CA 90067, tel: 866-446 6625; www.crystal cruises.com.

Cunard Line, US: 24305 Town Center Drive, Santa Clarita, CA 91355, tel: 661-753 1000. UK: Carnival House, 100 Harbour Parade, Southampton, SO15 1ST, tel: 0845 678 00 13; www.cunard.co.uk.

Disney Cruise Line, US: Disney Cruise Vacations, Guest Communications, PO Box 10238, Lake Buena Vista, FL 32830-0238; tel: 0800 028 3179; www.disneycruise.disney.go.com.

Fred Olsen Cruise Lines, UK: Fred Olsen House, Whitehouse Road, Ipswich, Suffolk IP1 5LL, tel: 01473 746175; www.fredolsen cruises.com.

Holland America Line, US: 300 Elliott Avenue West, Seattle, WA 98119, tel: +1 877-932 4259. UK: 5 Gainsford Street, London SE1 2NE, tel: 0845 351 0557; www.hollandamerica.com.

Norwegian Cruise Line, US: 7665 Corporate Center Drive, Miami, FL 33126, tel: 866-234 7350; www.ncl.com. UK: Horatio House, 77–85 Fulham Palace Road, London, W6 8JA, tel: 0845 201 8900; www.ncl.co.uk.

Oceania Cruises: 8300 NW 33rd Street, Suite 308, Miami, FL 33122, tel: 305-514 2300; www.oceaniacruises.com. UK: tel: 0845 505 1920; www.oceaniacruises.co.uk.

P&O Cruises, Carnival House, 100 Harbour Parade, Southampton, SO15 1ST, tel: 0845 678 0014; www.pocruises.com.

Princess Cruises, US: 24844 Avenue Rockefeller, Santa Clarita, CA 91355, tel: 800-774 6327. UK: Carnival House, 100 Harbour Parade, Southampton, SO15 1ST, tel: 0845 355 5800; www.princess.com.

Regent Seven Seas Cruises, US: 8300 NW 33rd Street, Suite 308, Miami, FL 33122, tel: 800-285 1835. UK: Beresford House,

Town Quay, Southampton, SO14 2AQ, tel: 02380 682 280; www. rssc.com.

Royal Caribbean International, US: 1050 Caribbean Way, Miami, FL 33132, tel: 866-562 7625. UK: Royal Caribbean Cruise Line, Building 2, Aviator Park, Station Road, Addlestone, Weybridge, Surrey KT15 2PG, tel: 0844 493 4005; www.royalcaribbean.co.uk.

Seabourn, US: 300 Elliott Avenue West, Seattle, WA 98119, tel: 800 929 9391. UK: Carnival House, 100 Harbour Parade, Southampton, SO15 1ST, tel: 0845 070 0500; www.seabourn.com

SeaDream Yacht Club, US: 601 Brickell Key Drive Suite 1050 Miami, FL 33131 tel: 800 707 4911. UK tel: 0800 783 1373; www. seabourn.com.

Silversea Cruises, US: 110 East Broward Blvd., Fort Lauderdale, FL 33301, tel: 800 722 9955. UK: 77–79 Great Eastern Street, London EC2A 3HU, tel: 0844 770 9030; www.silversea.com.

Star Clippers, US: 760 NW 107th Ave, Miami, FL 33172, tel: 800-442 0551. UK: c/o Fred Olsen, Fred Olsen House, Whitehouse Road, Ipswich, Suffolk IP1 5LL, tel: 0845 200 1645; www.star clippers.co.uk.

Thomson, UK: Thomson Cruise Service Centre, Mariner Street, Swansea SA1 5BA, tel: 0844 871 0872; www.thomson.co.uk/cruise.

Windstar Cruises, US: 2101 4th Avenue, Suite 210, Seattle WA 7245. UK: c/o Cruise Portfolio, 50–51 Wells Street, London, W1T 3PP, tel: 020 7434 0089; www.windstarcruises.com.

TOURIST INFORMATION

For more information about individual islands contact the local tourist offices, or the **Caribbean Tourism Organization,** Canada: 2 Bloor Street West, Suite 2601, Toronto, ON M4W 3E2, tel: 416-935 0767; www.onecaribbean.org. UK: 22 The Quadrant, Richmond, Surrey TW9 1BP; tel: 020 8948 0057; www.caribbean.co.uk. US: 80 Broad Street, Suite 3200, New York, NY 10004; tel: 212-635 9530; www.onecaribbean.org.

INDEX

Ambergris Caye (Belize) 54
Anthony's Key Resort (Roatán) 55
Antigua 18, 88, 107–11
Aruba & Curaçao 154, 164–8

Bahamas, the 58–65
Baie Orientale (St Martin) 100
Barbados 8, 9, 12, 21, 88, 138–46
Basseterre (St Kitts) 103
Bathsheba (Barbados) 3, 146
Belize 52, 51–4
    Belize City (Belize) 51, 53
Bequia 150
Boiling Lake (Dominica) 122–3
Bridgetown (Barbados) 138, 142–4
Brighton Beach (Barbados) 141
Brimstone Hill National Park (St Kitts) 105
British Virgin Islands 88, 94–6
Buccoo Reef (Tobago) 163

Cane Garden Bay (Tortola, BVI) 95–6
Cancún (Mexico) 44

Caneel Bay (St John, USVI) 93
Carib Indians 118, 121
Casa de Campo (Dominican Republic) 82
Castries (St Lucia) 132–3
Cayman Islands 69
Charlestown (Nevis) 106
Charlotte Amalie (St Thomas, USVI) 90–91
Charlotteville (Tobago) 163
Chichén Itzá (Mexico) 47–8
Christiansted (St Croix, USVI) 93
Colombier (St-Barthélemy) 103
Costa Maya (Mexico) 48–9
Costa Rica 52, 56–7
Cozumel (Mexico) 40, 42–3
Crown Point (Tobago) 163
Cuba 14, 15, 66, 67–9
Curaçao 154, 164, 166–7

Dominica 18, 88, 118–23
Dominican Republic 14, 15, 66, 81–2
El Luquillo Beach (Puerto Rico) 86

Everglades National Park, Florida (USA) 27

Falmouth (Jamaica) 75
Florida (USA) 8, 9, 21–34
Folkestone Marine Park and Visitors Centre (Barbados) 145
Fort-de-France (Martinique) 125–6
Fort Lauderdale (USA) 22, 28–31
Fort St Louis (Martinique) 128
Frederiksted (St Croix, USVI) 93
Freeport (Grand Bahama) 63
Freeport (Jamaica) 74
Friar's Bay (St Kitts) 106
Frigate Bay (St Kitts) 105

Galveston (USA) 21, 22, 36–7
George Town (Grand Cayman) 70–71
Grand Anse (Grenada) 155
Grand Bahama (The Bahamas) 58, 62–5
Grand Cayman 66, 69–71
Grande Anse (Guadeloupe) 116
Grenada 151–5
Guadeloupe 12, 15, 18, 88, 112–17

Gustavia (St Barthélemy)
    101–2

Havana (Cuba) 68
Honduras 52, 54
Houston (USA) 21, 22, 37

Indian River (Dominica)
    123

Jamaica 12, 16, 66, 73–80
Jost Van Dyke (BVI) 94,
    97

Key West (USA) 22, 37–8
Kingstown (St Vincent)
    140
Kohunlich (Mexico) 50

Lamanai (Belize) 54
La Romana (Dominican
    Republic) 81
La Soufrière volcano
    (Guadeloupe) 116
La Soufrière volcano (St
    Vincent) 150
Limón (Costa Rica) 56–7

Marigot (St Martin) 100
Marigot Bay (St Lucia)
    136
Martinique 88, 124–31
Mayreau 151
Mexico 8, 9, 11, 40,
    41–50
Miami (USA) 21–7
Montego Bay (Jamaica)
    73, 74–5
Mustique 151

Nassau (the Bahamas)
    60–2
Nevis 106
New Orleans (USA) 21,
    22, 35
New Providence Island
    (the Bahamas) 58,
    59–62

Ocho Rios (Jamaica) 71,
    76–7
Oranjestad (Aruba) 164
Orlando (USA) 32

Palm Beach (Aruba) 165
Paradise Island (the
    Bahamas) 60, 62
Philipsburg (Sint
    Maarten) 96–9
Pigeon Point (Tobago)
    163
Pitons, The (St Lucia)
    132, 134
Playa del Carmel
    (Mexico) 40, 44–5
Pointe-à-Pitre
    (Guadeloupe) 18,
    113–15
Ponce (Puerto Rico) 86
Port Antonio (Jamaica)
    73, 79
Port Canaveral (USA) 22,
    31
Port Elizabeth (Bequia)
    150–51
Port of Spain (Trinidad)
    158–60
Portsmouth (Dominica)
    119, 123

Puerto Costa Maya
    (Mexico) 40, 48
Puerto Rico 8, 12, 14, 21,
    66, 83–86
Puerto Viejo de Limón
    (Costa Rica) 57

Road Town (Tortola, BVI)
    95
Roatán 52, 55–6
Roseau (Dominica) 119,
    120–21

St-Barthélemy 100–01
St Croix (US Virgin
    Islands) 87, 93
St George's (Grenada)
    152–3
St Jean (St-Barthélemy)
    102
St John (US Virgin
    Islands) 87, 92–3
St John's (Antigua)
    107–10
St Kitts 12, 88, 103–6
St Lucia 13, 88, 131–38
St-Martin 88 99–100
St-Pierre (Martinique)
    129–30
St Thomas (US Virgin
    Islands) 89–92
St Vincent & The
    Grenadines 148–50
San José (Costa Rica) 57
San Juan (Puerto Rico)
    21, 84–6
San Miguel (Cozumel) 42
Santo Domingo
    (Dominican Republic)

12, 81
Scarborough (Tobago)
    161
Shell Beach
    (St-Barthélemy) 100
Sint Maarten 88, 97
Soufrière (St Lucia)
    135
Spanish Town (Virgin
    Gorda, BVI) 96
Speightstown (Barbados)
    145

Speyside (Tobago) 163

Tampa (USA) 33
Tobago 154, 162–3
Tortola (BVI) 94, 95–6
Trinidad & Tobago 154,
    158–63

US Virgin Islands 89–93
Valley of Desolation (Do-
    minica) 122
Venezuela 11, 167

Virgin Gorda (BVI) 96
Virgin Islands see British
    Virgin Islands, US
    Virgin Islands

Willemstad (Curaçao)
    166–7
Xcaret (Mexico) 45–6
Xuanantunich (Belize) 54

Yucatán Peninsula
    (Mexico) 41–42

Berlitz pocket guide

Caribbean Ports of Call

Second Edition 2011

Written by Sarah Cameron
Edited by Paula Soper
Series Editor: Tom Stainer

No part of this book may be reproduced,
stored in a retrieval system or transmitted
in any form or means photocopying, recording or
mechanical, photocopying, recording or
otherwise, without prior written permission
from Berlitz Publishing. Brief text
quotations with use of photographs are
exempted for book review purposes only.
Every effort has been made to provide
accurate information in this publication,
but changes are inevitable. The publisher
cannot be responsible for any resulting
loss, inconvenience or injury.

Photography credits
AWL Images, 2BL; Alamy 101, 116; Anse
castanet Resort 133; Antigua and Barbuda
Tourist office 108, 110; Aruba Tourist
Authority 164; Bahamas Tourist Office 59, 63;
Barbados Tourism Authority 4TL, 138, 139,
143, 147; Belize Tourist Board/Demian Solano
2TL; Pete Bennett 37, 59; Laurent

Benoit/Comite du tourisme de Saint
Barthelemy 4BL; BVI Tourist Board 94; Blount
Small Ship 20; Cayman Islands Dept of
Tourism 70; Kevin Cummins 73, 74, 77, 78, 79,
80; Curacao Tourist Board 166; Jerry Dennis
109; Discover Dominica Authority 119, 120;
Jurg Donatsch 168; Mary Evans 13; Glynn
Genin 14, 23, 25, 85, 86; Philippe Giraud for
The Guadeloupe Island Tourist Board 115,
116; Grenada Board of Tourism 155, 156; Tony
Halliday 50; Alex Havret 3TL, 5BR, 6B, 41, 43,
44, 45, 47, 48, 64, 68; Ariane Hunter 158;
iStock 2TR, 3BR, 3CL, 3CR, 4-5B, 4BC, 4TR,
5BC, 5TL, 5TR, 6C, 6T, 7T, 10, 19, 34, 61, 62,
82, 87, 89, 90, 92, 94, 96, 97, 102, 104, 112,
116, 123, 131, 135, 140, 145, 148, 163; Nevis
Tourism Authority 106, 107; Richard Nowitz
27, 29, 30, 33, 39; Luc Olivier/Martinique
Tourist Board 124, 125, 126; Photolibrary 55;
Sylvaine Pointau 7B, 15, 26, 67, 146; Mark
Read 31; St Lucia Tourist board 136; St
Maarten Tourist Board 16, 98; Corrie Wingate
3TR, 7C, 8BL, 51, 53, 54, 57; St.Vincent & the
Grenadines Tourist Office/Chris Caldicott 151;
Trinidad & Tobago Tourism Development
Company 160; US Virgin Islands Tourism 87;
Bill Wassman 147; Phil Wood 71.
Cover picture: 4Corners Images

Contact us

At Berlitz we strive to keep our guides as
accurate and up to date as possible, but if you
find anything that has changed, or if you have
any suggestions on ways to improve this guide,
then we would be delighted to hear from you.
Berlitz Publishing, PO Box 7910,
London SE1 1WE, England.
email: berlitz@apaguide.co.uk
www.berlitzpublishing.com